Life in Upper Canada
1781-1841

Curriculum Resource Books Series

GENERAL EDITOR
Mollie E. Cottingham, M.A.
Faculty of Education
University of British Columbia

1. **Today's World**
Selected Sources —
from 1688 to Modern Times
J. Arthur Lower

2. **The New World**
Selected Sources — Canada,
the United States and
Latin America to 1914
Patricia M. Johnson

3. **The First Million Years**
Selected Sources — from
Prehistory to the Christian Era
Mollie E. Cottingham

4. **East and West**
Selected Sources — from the
Fall of Rome to 1700
Mollie E. Cottingham

5. **British Columbia**
An Introduction to
Geographic Studies
J. V. Horwood

6. **The Landscape of Europe**
Four Geographic Studies
James Popple

7. **Canada's Pacific Province**
Selected Sources — British
Columbia from Early Times
Patricia M. Johnson

8. **Self-Government**
Selected Sources in the History
of the Commonwealth
J. Arthur Lower

9. **Renaissance to Revolution**
Selected Historical Sources
Mollie E. Cottingham and
J. Arthur Lower

10. **Canada Since 1867**
Selected Historical Sources
Patricia M. Johnson

11. **The Northland**
Studies of the Yukon and the
Northwest Territories
John Wolforth

12. **Confederation 1867**
Selected Sources — from
Durham's Report to the
British North America Act
Thomas F. Bredin

13. **Adolescents in Society**
Selected Sources in Personal
and Social Relationships
Anne McCreary-Juhasz and
George Szasz

14. **The Prairies**
Selected Historical Sources
Kenneth Osborne

15. **Careers Today**
Selected Sources
Joan Morris

16. **Nationalism to Internationalism**
Selected Sources — from
1844 to Modern Times
J. Arthur Lower

17. **Industrialization and Society**
Selected Sources
Gerald Walsh

18. **The Family**
Selected Sources
Phyllis J. Meiklejohn

19. **Black and White in North America**
Selected Sources
Terence D. Tait

20. **Communities in Canada**
Selected Sources
Leonard Marsh

21. **Patterns of Settlement in Southern Ontario**
Three Studies
R. C. Langman

22. **China in the Twentieth Century**
Selected Sources
Jason Wong

23. **Indians in Transition**
Selected Sources
Gerald Walsh

24. **Life in Upper Canada 1781-1841**
An Inquiry Approach
Dean Fink

Life in Upper Canada 1781-1841

An Inquiry Approach

DEAN FINK

*Lord Elgin High School,
Burlington, Ontario*

MCCLELLAND AND STEWART LIMITED

Contents

Preface

Henry Ford, the automotive magnate, once said that "history is bunk." Many students of Canadian history not only agree with this view, but go one step further by describing Canadian history as dull bunk. By using the tools of historians and social scientists this book will hopefully encourage the student to examine a wide variety of sources, develop his own interpretations based upon evidence, and evaluate conflicting attitudes and values. By applying these techniques to an epoque in Canadian history, students can become aware of both the relevance and fascination of history in general and Canadian history in particular.

The history of Upper Canada fulfills these criteria admirably. Born out of the defeat of the British Loyalists in the American Revolution, Upper Canada, until its disappearance as a distinct colony in 1841, provides insight into the values and attitudes which make up the English-Canadian character. While the Upper Canadian political scene is both interesting and vital to an understanding of the period, the political situation is in many ways only a reflection of social, economic, religious, and educational attitudes and values. For this reason, selections in this book have emphasized these latter aspects without totally ignoring political factors.

The subtitle *An Inquiry Approach*, reflects the book's fundamental purpose, that of promoting critical thinking. While many books set out with the intention of developing this faculty, most fail in their objective, in the sense that they merely exercise the student's memory.

In an attempt to combat this approach, the questions throughout the book have been set to precede the selections. This has been done in order to encourage the analysis, restructuring, and reorganization of materials so that the student may create new patterns, and then evaluate materials, ideas or values upon a basis of clearly defined criteria.

This book does not pretend to cover all the issues of the period nor does it attempt to provide a chronological narrative of Upper Canada. It should therefore be used in concert with a text which will provide a useful overview and review. When you have finished studying *Upper Canada*, it is hoped that you will think of history as interesting and thought-provoking.

ONE

The Loyalists c. 1781-1791

". . . traversing these bloody Fields, where many
brave and generous men have met their Fate, my
Imagination, touched as I was with my own Circumstances, represented to me in the most affecting
Colours the Unhappiness of the different surviving
Relations. The weeping Parent, distressed Widow,
wretched Orphans, and afflicted Friends seeing to
present themselves to my revolving mind drew from
me with a Sigh, O cursed ambition, what Miseries
dost thou bring upon Mankind! Perhaps the woes
of others then most affect us, when our Heart is
softened by feelings arising from our own Condition."[1]

This anguished cry of the political fugitive is timeless. He
could be a Czech fleeing from Russian tanks, a Jew from Gestapo
gas chambers, or a Vietnamese from a firing squad. This tor-
mented refugee, however, was Richard Cartwright, an American
Tory, or as Canadians would identify him, an United Empire
Loyalist. Born in 1759 in the state of New York, he found himself caught up in the chaotic events of the American Revolution.
"The distracted Condition of my native Country," he wrote in
1779 "where all Government was subverted, where Caprice was
the only rule and measure of usurped Authority, and where all
the Distress was exhibited that Power guided by Malice can produce . . ." forced him, along with thousands of others who supported Britain's attempts to maintain her empire and prevent
American independence, "to quit a Place where Discord reigned
and all miseries of anarchy had long prevailed."[2]

By "quitting" this "Place," Cartwright and his fellow Loyalists found permanent settlements in what is now Ontario and
helped to shape every aspect of life in Upper Canada. In fact
their numbers and influence made the creation of this colony a
reality in 1791.

The Loyalist era like any historical period, breeds controversy,
because the study of history is itself subject to interpretation and

[1] J. J. Talman, *Loyalist Narratives From Upper Canada* (Toronto:
Champlain Society, 1946), p. 47.
[2] J. J. Talman, *Ibid.*, pp. 45-46.

therefore controversy. To gain further insight into the nature of history and the history of the Loyalists in particular, let us begin where a historian begins, with questions.

1.   Identifying the Problems

1. List the problems or questions about the Loyalists raised by the following selection of sources.

2. Account for the difference in the way Ryerson looks upon the Loyalists and the way the Albany newspaper views these same refugees.

3. Why is it necessary to examine the publishing place and date of each source?

4. Which of the following views does your Canadian history textbook tend to support?

1) . . . In no country upon the face of the Globe, and at no period in the history of any country, has appeared a higher or purer order of patriotism, than is written upon the pages of the history of British America. British connection is to mostly every son of the land dearer ever than life itself. At least, it has been so in respect to those of whom we write, the U. E. Loyalists. Co-equal with the love they have to the British Crown, is the hearty aversion they bear to Republicanism[1] . . . . The U. E. Loyalists have been a barrier of rock against which the waves of Republicanism have dashed in vain. . . .

> William Canniff, *A History of the Settlement of Upper Canada* (Toronto, 1869), pp. 633-634.

2) As Hannibal swore never to be at Peace with the Romans, so let every Whig sware – by the abhorence of Slavery – by the liberty and religion . . . by everything that a free man holds dear – never to be at peace with those fiends the Refugees, whose thefts, murders and treasons, have filled the cup of woe; but shew the world that we prefer War, with all its dreadful calamities, to giving those self-destroyers of the human species a residence among us. – We have crimsoned the earth with our blood to purchase peace, therefore are determined to enjoy harmony uninterrupted with the Contaminating breath of a Tory.

> Extract from an Albany, New York, newspaper, May 26, 1783, quoted in Hazel C. Mathews, *The Mark of Honour* (Toronto: University of Toronto Press, 1965), appendix D.

[1] Republicanism refers to the American democratic system where the Head of State is the President rather than a Monarch.

3) . . . the history of the Loyalists of America has never been written except by their enemies and spoilers, and those English historians who have not troubled themselves with examining original authorities, but have adopted the authorities, and in some instances imbibed the spirit of American historians, who have never tired in eulogizing Americans and everything American, and deprecating everything English, and all who have adhered loyally to the unity of the British Empire.

> Egerton Ryerson, *The Loyalists of America and Their Times* (Toronto, 1880), Vol. I, p. iii.

4) Since land was made available on much easier terms to Loyalists than to other settlers, as many newcomers as could possibly do so, regardless of their background, claimed to be Loyalists. In fact after 1784 it is very difficult to separate "land hunger" from "loyalty" a cause for immigration to the region adjacent to Lakes Erie and Ontario, particularly with respect to the "late Loyalists." This situation prevailed even after a great effort had been made to purge these people's names from the Loyalist lists.

> R. O. MacFarlane, "The Loyalist Migrations: A Social and Economic Movement," *Manitoba Essays* (Winnipeg, 1937), pp. 107-108.

5) In fairness to the Loyalists it must be said that it was their support of Britain which brought them into the position of finding themselves astride a rail or unable to remain in their own communities . . . .

Generalizations regarding the motives of the Loyalists are dangerous: but it seems fair to say that the great majority of the first emigrants from the thirteen colonies went to Canada because their actions or words had made it impossible for them to remain in, or return to, their pre-revolutionary homes.

> J. J. Talman, *op. cit.*, p. xxvii.

2.   Loyalist Motives

By 1780, American successes forced increasing numbers of Loyalists to abandon homes and migrate to British territory at Three Rivers and Sorel in Quebec. The provincial governor, General Frederick Haldimand, and his immediate superior Sir Guy Carleton, Commander in Chief of British forces, faced the difficult task of handling the Loyalist influx.

1. Why does Carleton feel the Loyalists migrated to Canada?

2. How does Carleton propose to treat these people? What policy was, in fact, pursued?

3. In addition to Canada, where else might Loyalists go to avoid "suffering" at American hands?

1) From Sir Guy Carleton to General Haldimand, New York, June 4, 1783

Sir

The Condition of His Majesty's Faithful Subjects who have been driven from their Estates, and have suffered every other Inconvenience on account of their Loyalty and Services, demands the most benevolent Consideration. –

Many Thousands of these have already been induced to seek an Asylum in Nova Scotia . . . .

There are others, Sir, of the above description in Number about Two Hundred Families as I am informed who wish to pass into Canada, & find Grants and Habitations there, and I think it my Duty, Sir, to recommend in the strongest Terms to your Excellency's Consideration, the making Grants of Land to those Persons in the Neighbourhood of frontenac, where they are desirous to settle, and without any Reservation of Rents or the Payment of any Fees or Expences whatever, to which I hope your Excellency will add Aid of a years Provisions in like manner as has been given in Nova Scotia, as also other Aids and Assistance within your Power, & as the Necessities of these deserving People in their Condition of Settlers may require, they being undoubtedly entitled to all the Protection and Assistance we can give them.

Public Archives of Canada, Haldimand MSS., B146, pp. 63-64.

3.   The Loyalists and the Thirteen Colonies

1. Consider to what extent the following sources provide evidence to support Carleton's view of the Loyalists' motives.

2. Do these sources suggest any other motives for the Loyalist exodus?

3. To this point how would you answer the question, "Why did the Loyalists come to Canada?"

1) Yesterday, about noon, an effigy of Governor Tryon[1] was exhibited through the principal parts of New York City, attended by a great concourse of the inhabitants and others . . . .

After it had been sufficiently exposed, it was hung on a gallows, which had been prepared in the middle of the parade, where, after having received the

[1] William Tryon, the Royal Governor of New York, led Loyalist forces against the American rebels.

contempt of an oppressed, insulted, and incensed people, it was cut down and destroyed, the whole being conducted without any manner of injury to any person whatever, unless it was to the person who kept the sign of Tryon's Arms, which were taken down by some of the procession.

> Frank Moore, *Diary of the American Revolution* 2 vols., (New York: C. Scribner, 1860), I, pp. 223-225.

2) August 8 [1775] – The riflemen on their way from the southern colonies through the country, administer the new-fashioned discipline of tar and feathers to the obstinate and refractory Tories that they meet on their road, which has a very good effect. Those whose crimes are of a more atrocious nature, they punish by sending them to General Gage.[1] They took a man in New Melford, Connecticut, a most incorrigible Tory, who called them d—d rebels, etc., and made him walk before them to Litchfield, which is twenty miles, and carry one of his own geese all the way in his hand. When they arrived there, they tarred him, and make him pluck his goose, and then bestowed the feathers on him, drummed him out of the company, and obliged him to kneel down and thank them for their lenity.

3) The whole city was searched for "tories," and several were dragged "from their lurking holes, where they had taken refuge to avoid the undeserved vengeance of an ungovernable rabble." These "unhappy victims" were put "upon sharp rails with one leg on each side; each rail was carried upon the shoulders of two tall men, with a man on each side to keep the poor wretch straight and fixed in his seat." "Numbers" were thus paraded through the streets, and at every corner loudly denounced as notorious "tories."

> A. C. Flick, *Loyalism in New York* (New York: Columbia University Press, 1901), pp. 35-36.

4) Act for the Forfeiture and Sale of the Property of Loyalists: New York State, October 22, 1779

Whereas during the present unjust and cruel war waged by the king of Great Britain against this State, and the other United States of America, divers persons holding or claiming property within this State have voluntarily been adherent to the said King his fleets and armies, enemies to this State and the said other United States, with intent to subvert the government and liberties of this State and the said other United States, and to bring the same in subjection to the crown of Great Britain by reason whereof the said persons have severally justly forfeited all right to the protection of this State and to the benefit of the laws under which said property is held or claimed.

> A. C. Flick, ed., *The American Revolution in New York: Its Political and Social Significance* (Albany: The University of the State of New York, 1926), p. 348.

[1] General Thomas Gage was commander of British forces in America until 1775 when he was replaced by General Howe.

5) Testimonial of John Stuart[1]

My House has been frequently broken open by Mobs; – my Property plundered, and indeed every Kind of Indignity offered to my Person by the lowest of the Populace; – At length my Farm and the Produce of it was formally taken from me in May last, as forfeited to the State, and as the last Resource I proposed to open a Latin School for the Support of my Family; But this Privilege was denied, on Pretence that as a Prisoner of War, I was not intitled to exercise any lucrative Occupation in the State. I then applied for Permission to remove to Canada, which after much Difficulty & Expence I obtained upon the following Conditions: to give Bail in the sum of £400 to send a rebel Colonel in my Room, or else return to Albany, and surrender myself Prisoner whenever required. In Consequence of which, I set out on my Journey from Schenectady on the 19th of September last with my Wife & three small Children; and after suffering much Fatigue & Difficulty we arrived safe at St. John's in Canada on the 9th instant. The Mohawks are extremely happy at my Arrival, & flatter themselves that I will reside among them; But, having left the most Part of my private Property, by the depretiation of the Paper Currency & other Accidents peculiar to the Times, – And having a Family to maintain in this very expensive Place, I shall be under the Necessity of accepting of a Chaplaincy, which Sr. John Johnson[2] (with his wonted Kindness) is pleased to offer me in his Second Battalion.

I cannot omit to mention that my Church was plundered by the Rebels, & the Pulpit Cloth taken away from the Pulpit – it was afterwards imployed as a Tavern, the Barrel of Rum placed in the Reading Desk, – the succeeding Season it was used as a Stable – And now serves as a Fort to protect a Set of as great Villains as ever disgraced Humanity.

> As quoted in J. W. Lydekker, "The Reverend John Stuart, Missionary to the Mohawks," *Historical Magazine of the Protestant Episcopal Church*, Vol. II (March 1942), pp. 39-41.

6) Testimonial of Roger Bates[3]

Our family came originally from Yorkshire in England. They were of the old fashioned Tory or Conservative school, who looked upon no form of government equal to the British constitution founded on the principles laid down by the English Barons at Runnymeade, when they compelled King John to sign the Great Charter of Liberty.

To the present day, all the Bates family follow in the footsteps of their Ancestors.

As encouragement was held out for Loyal British settlers to locate in

[1] The first Anglican clergyman in Upper Canada.

[2] Sir John Johnson (1742-1830) organized two battalions of the King's Royal Regiment of New York which was active in the border warfare of the American Revolution. In 1783 he was appointed Superintendent General and Inspector of Indian Affairs in British North America.

[3] Roger Bates was a farmer near Cobourg.

America, my grandfather turned his attention to the Western Hemisphere, and having satisfied his mind that his posterity might become considerable land-owners, he sailed for the New World, and arrived in Boston between the years 1760 and 1770, when he commenced farming, lands at that period being obtained at a very low price to actual settlers.

The troubles commenced in 1774, when all who were loyal to the House of Hanover,[1] took up arms in defence of their Sovereign. In this conflict, my grandfather took a conspicuous part. My grandmother was an active intelligent woman, wonderfully industrious, who attended to the farming affairs till they were compelled to quit the United States Territory being determined never to side with the Republicans. Liberal offers were made to the U. E. Loyalists so the family removed their effects to Upper Canada, where for their services the Governor granted them 1200 acres of land and 200 acres for each of the children.

> "Testimony of Roger Bates," *Ontario Historical Society*, Vol. X
> (Toronto, 1906), pp. 146-153.

4.   Reassessment

1. In section three you were asked to give a tentative answer to the question, why did the Loyalists come to Canada? Your answer is, in effect, an hypothesis concerning the Loyalists' motives. After reading the following sources, how would you restate your hypothesis?

2. Having examined a variety of sources, which view, concerning the Loyalists' motives stated in section two, appears valid? Why?

3. What further steps would you take to prove or validate your hypothesis?

1) **Anonymous Petition** (Circulated among Loyalists at Sorel)

Copy of the form of a petition . . . and Circulated . . . throughout the different Cantonments of the Loyalists in Canada. Dated at Quebec the 24th April 1784.

After the form or Caption let them say they don't chuse[2] that Lands at Cataraque[3] or the Bay of Chaleurs[4] on the terms offered, and that the Declaration put down in Lorth North's[5] instructions to General Haldimand to be signed by every one taking lands is unconstitutional, that they have a right to refuse it . . . we have endeavoured to use all endeavours to keep up the British Constitution, have sacrificed all our Property and ventured our Lives, and our

[1] The British monarchy.
[2] choose, [3] present day Kingston, [4] In New Brunswick,
[5] British Secretary for the Home Department.

poor familys are now beggars for our Loyalty but still will would take Arms again in the same Cause if the King would allow us Arms, which we have been deprived of by General Haldimand's order after using them in His Majesty's service or for several years we expect to be Subsisted in Any of the King's Dominions where we settel until we can subsist ourselves which we have the promise of from the King – this will not be long we will be diligent and industrious, and want only a reasonable time. Utensils we want &c. and think it a little hard that we are obliged to take the King's Land under on worse terms than we can get it under the French Seigniors[1] in Canada. . . . Don't let us be disheartened or be made slaves of in this Province, let us stand for our rights we have the King & Parliament and a British Constitution we will maintain with our lives and fortune. Loyalists it is now for you to shew the world you have a feeling for Britain & yourselves draw up a petition to the Commr in Chief of what you wishes are send it to A.Z. Quebec . . . .

P.A.C., Haldimand MSS., B178, pp. 289-291.

2) Letter of Richard Cartwright to His Excellency General Hunter

Kingston, 23rd August, 1799.

Sir, – . . . Your Excellency is already aware that the settlement of this Province was originally suggested by the propriety and necessity of providing an asylum for the American Loyalists after the peace of 1783. Those who were already in the Province of Quebec were afterwards joined by a considerable number from New York, who preferred this country to Nova Scotia, and there were further added to them several of the German troops, and some of the disbanded soldiers of the British regiments. . . . For the four first years the strictest attention was paid, not to admit any other description of persons as settlers; but in the year 1788 some little relaxation took place in this particular, and it having been represented to Lord Dorchester[2] that there were in the States many relations of the Loyalists as well as other persons, who, although they had not joined the Royal standard, were, however, well affected to the British Government, his Lordship was pleased to give it as an instruction to the Boards . . . to examine into the loyalty and good character of such persons as were disposed to become settlers, and if they appeared to be unexceptionable in these respects, to give them a certificate of location for a lot of not more than two hundred acres, under the express condition of becoming *bona fide* settlers. Thus many useful inhabitants were gradually acquired, ... In this train affairs continued till this country was made a separate Province, and General Simcoe[3] sent over to govern it. He appears to have thought that the immediate peopling of the country was an object of sufficient importance to supersede the regulations which had been hitherto observed in distributing the waste lands of the Crown. A proclamation was immediately issued for the

[1] Seigniors were Frenchmen who had received land from the French King.
[2] Sir Guy Carleton who returned to Canada as Governor in 1786.
[3] John Graves Simcoe, Upper Canada's first Lieutenant-Governor (1791-1796).

purpose of inviting emigrants, and the speculations in lands being about this time at their height in the American States, jobbers[1] flocked in from every quarter, proposing to bring a large number of settlers, and the Loyalists heard, with astonishment and indignation, persons spoken of as proprietors of townships whom they had encountered in the field under the banners of the rebellion, or who had been otherwise notoriously active in promoting the American revolution. . . . I will not disguise from your Excellency the opinion which I have always entertained, and on every proper occasion expressed, that this ought never to have been permitted. One necessary consequence has been to dispel the opinion fondly cherished by the Loyalists, that the donation of lands to them in this country was intended as a mark of peculiar favour and a reward for their attachment to their Sovereign; for how could such an idea remain upon their minds, when they afterwards saw them lavished upon persons who had such pretensions? . . . .

Cartwright, C. E., ed., *Life and Letters of the Late Hon. Richard Cartwright* (Toronto, 1876), pp. 83-95.

5. The Loyalists' Identity and Patterns of Settlement

From the preceding selections it became evident that a wide variety of backgrounds existed among the Loyalists such as government officials, large and small landowners, artisans, doctors, lawyers and clergymen. This of course raises questions concerning which of these elements came to Upper Canada.

1. What occupational elements seem to predominate among Loyalists?

2. Account for the type of Loyalist who came to Upper Canada.

1) Col. Dundas[2] to Lord Cornwallis[3]

Montreal, 3rd October, 1787.

My Lord, – I had the honour of writing to your Lordship in the month of November last from the province of New Brunswick. Mr. Pemberton, my colleague, and I, having finished the business of the Commission in those parts, we came to Canada in the month of May, and have been employed all this summer in examining the claims of persons resident in this extensive country. They are very numerous – I think from 1100 to 1200 – but are in amount

[1] land speculators
[2] Commissioner investigating Loyalist claims.
[3] Former British military leader during the revolutionary war later became Governor-General of India (1786-1793).

very small, being mostly farmers from the back parts of New York Province. These people have been settled since the peace in the upper part of Canada, beginning 50 miles above Montreal, and extending to Niagara. They find the soil excellent and the climate good. They are mostly thriving, in so much that already they have been able to supply the King's posts with bread, . . .

Canada, my lord, has surprised me very much, as I had figured to myself that it resembled Nova Scotia; but it is, particularly near this place, equal in extent of rich country to any part of America. The winter is long, but still the summers are sufficient to ripen any grain. The Canadians are in number about 120,000; the Loyalists are about 6,000, and they are a happy, flourishing people.

Ontario Bureau of Archives, 1904, pp. 22-23.

2) Extract from a Letter from Lieut. Governor Hope[1] to the Commissioners for American Claims

dated Quebec 29th January 1786.

The Loyalists in this Province, with a few exceptions do not consist of Persons of great Property or consequence. They are chiefly Landholders, Farmers and others from the Inland parts of the Continent, many of whom very early quitted their homes and Possessions to join the Royal Standard, the rest have been forced to abandon them and take refuge under His Majestys Government. – Their Claims to Compensation cannot singly be considerable. The indulgences which have been bestowed, by Allotting Lands for their improvement, and allowing Provisions for their Support, assisted by the active and persevering Exertions of their own Industry, have already procured for them promising Settlements – A small compensation for their Losses would restore to the greater part of them all the Comforts and Conveniences they have lost, but if those are only to be obtained by quitting the Establishments their Industry has secured, for such a length of time as a Voyage to and from Halifax would require, the sacrifice is too great.

By the Muster rolls of Loyalists settled in this Province taken in the Months of August, September and October last, The total Numbers are about Six Thousand three hundred exclusive of about Five Hundred settled in Chaleur and Gaspé Bays in the Lt. Government of Gaspé.

The *Heads* of families are about two Thousand five hundred, who are distributed nearly as follows

near Niagara and Detroit	300
from Johnstown to Cataraqui & its Vicinity	1800
about Sorel and in all the lower Canada	200
Chaleur Bay and Gaspé	200
	2500

E. A. Cruikshank, ed., *Records of Niagara 1784-1787* (Niagara-on-the-Lake: Niagara Historical Society, Publications, No. 39, 1928), p. 80.

[1] Lieutenant-Governor of the province of Quebec, which in 1786 included the territory of Upper Canada.

To this point our pursuit of the identity of the Loyalists has been of a general nature, now our task is to be more precise.

1. From the following source, determine what organizational patterns were to be pursued in settling the Loyalists.

2. By comparing the numbers involved in the following sources, with Carleton's estimate in section two, what conclusions can be drawn?

3. How does this source alter your initial impressions of the Loyalists' identity?

3) The Settlement of The United Empire Loyalists

These begin at No. 1, Lake St. Francis going upwards. Montreal, July, 1784.	MEN	WOMEN	CHILDREN	SERVANTS	TOTAL
1st Battalion, late King's Royal Rgt., N. York and those attached settled on Townships Nos. 1, 2, 3, 4, and 5	549	257	631	25	1462
Part of Major Jessup's corps and those attached, settled on Townships Nos. 6 and 7 and part of 8	187	85	211	12	495
2nd Battalion, late King's Royal Rgt., N. York and those attached, settled on Townships Nos. 3 and 4 Cataraqui	199	32	69	10	310
Capt. Grass's party and those attached, on Tp.[1] No. 1 Cataraqui[2]	88	33	66	....	187
Part of Major Jessup's and those attached, settled on Township No. 2, Cataraqui	137	71	214	12	434
Major Roger's corps and those attached, settled on Tp. No. 3, Cataraqui	120	47	118	14	299
Major Van Alstine's party of Loyalists settled on Tp. No. 4, Cataraqui	92	46	103	17	253
Different detachments of disbanded Regular Regiments settled on Tp. No. 5, Cataraqui	153	39	67	....	259
Detachment of Germans with Baron Reitzenstein, settled on Tp. No. 5, Cataraqui	30	8	6	....	44
Rangers of the Six Nation Department and Loyalists settled With the Mohawk Indians at the Bay of Quinté	13	8	7	....	23
[1]Township [2]Kingston	1568	626	1492	90	3776

P.A.C. Haldimand Papers MSS., B168, p. 42.

Throughout the 1780's, Loyalists moved into the Cataraqui area, the Niagara Peninsula to the west, and the old French fort at Detroit even further to the west. Their numbers prevent identification, but by examining the case of one group it is possible to understand something of the problem. The following source examines the officers of Major Edward Jessup's Corps referred to in the previous reading.

1. To what extent does this source support or refute your previously held views on the Loyalists' identity?

2, What general statements can be made concerning occupations, places of birth, length of service, and national origins based on surnames?

3. What relationship, if any, exists between former occupation and rank in the service?

4) A Return of the Officers of the Loyal Rangers

RANK	NAME	PLACE OF BIRTH	TERM OF SERVICE
Major	Edw. Jessup	Conn.[1]	7 yrs.

Former Station and Remarks
A volunteer in the Seven Years' War. Commanded a company of Provincials in 1759. He was a Justice of the Peace in Albany County where he was a large property owner.

| Capt. | Eben. Jessup | Conn. | 7 yrs. |

He was a Justice of the Peace in Albany County and a large property owner. Served as lieut.-col. under Burgoyne. From 1777 he was paid as a captain. When the corps was reorganized in 1781 he was continued as a captain under his brother.

| Capt. | John Peters | Conn. | 7 yrs. |

He was a Justice of the Peace for Gloucester County. He owned property there. He was a lieut.-col. of a corps in 1777. Until 1781 he was paid as captain. When the Provincials were reorganized in 1781 he was made a captain in the Loyal Rangers.

| Capt. | Justus Sherwood | Conn. | 7 yrs. |

He was a farmer in the New Vermont State.

| Capt. | Jonathan Jones | Conn. | 7 yrs. |

He was a Justice of the Peace for Albany County where he had a farm, mills, and other property.

| Capt. | Wm. Fraser | Scotland | 6½ yrs. |

He was a farmer in New York.

| Capt. | John Jones | Conn. | 6½ yrs. |

He was a farmer in New York.

| Capt. | Peter Drummond | Scotland | 7 yrs. |

He was a farmer in New York.

[1] Connecticut.

RANK	NAME	PLACE OF BIRTH	TERM OF SERVICE
Capt.	John W. Meyers	N.Y. Province	6½ yrs.
	He was a farmer in New York.		
Capt.	Thos. Fraser	Scotland	6½ yrs.
	He was a farmer in New York.		
Lieut.	Guisbert Sharp	N.Y. Province	6½ yrs.
	He was a wealthy farmer.		
Lieut.	Henry Simmonds	N.Y. Province	6½ yrs.
	He was a farmer.		
Lieut.	David Jones	Conn.	7 yrs.
	He was a farmer in New York.		
Lieut.	Alex Campbell	N.Y. Province	6½ yrs.
	He was a farmer in New York.		
Lieut.	James Parrot	Boston Province	7 yrs.
	He was a farmer in New York.		
Lieut.	David McFall	Ireland	7 yrs.
	He was a sergeant in the 26th regiment for many years and served seven years in the Provincial troops.		
Lieut.	John Dulmage	Conn.	7 yrs.
	He was a farmer in New York.		
Lieut.	Gershom French	Conn.	6½ yrs.
	He was a young man of some property and had just started up as a merchant when the revolution came.		
Lieut.	Gideon Adams	Conn.	7 yrs.
	He was a farmer.		
Lieut.	John Ritter (Ruyter)	N.Y. Province	6½ yrs.
	He was a farmer in New York province.		
Lieut.	James Robins	Old England	6½ yrs.
	He was a merchant in New York province.		
Lieut.	Edw. Jessup	N.Y. Province	6¼ yrs.
	He was a dependent on Major Jessup.		
Ensign	John Dusenbury	N.Y. Province	6½ yrs.
	He was a farmer's son.		
Ensign	John Peters	Conn.	6½ yrs.
	He was a dependent on Col. Peters.		
Ensign	Elijah Bottom	Conn.	6½ yrs.
	He was a farmer's son.		
Ensign	Thos. Sherwood	Conn.	4½ yrs.
	He was a farmer in New York.		
Ensign	Thos. Mann	N.Y. Province	6½ yrs.
	He was a farmer's son.		
Ensign	Harmonius Best	N.Y. Province	6½ yrs.
	He was a farmer.		

RANK	NAME	PLACE OF BIRTH	TERM OF SERVICE
Ensign	Wm. Lamson	Conn.	7 yrs.
	He was a farmer in New York.		
Ensign	Conrad Best	N.Y. Province	6 yrs.
	He was a farmer in New York.		
Adjutant	Matthew Thompson	Ireland	2 yrs.
	He had served many years in the 31st regiment where he was a sergeant-major. He served two years in the Provincial troops.		
Quarter-Master	John Ferguson	Ireland	1yr. 10 months
	He was a sergeant-major in the 29th regiment for many years. He served one year and ten months in the Provincial troops.		
Surgeon	George Smyth	Ireland	2½ yrs.
	He was a physician in New York province.		
Surgeon's Mate	Solomon Jones	Conn.	7 yrs.
	He was a student of his profession (medicine) in Albany, N.Y.		

Signed
Edw. Jessup,
Major Commandant Loyal Rangers

P.A.C., Haldimand MSS., B167, p. 398.

1. Upon what principle was land to be allotted?

2. Using this definition of a social class: "a large group of people who share many things in common and who are classified by other members of the community as belonging together," and examining previous readings, suggest what social classes might exist in the Loyalist communities and what criteria are used to place people in these social classes.

3. By checking these estimates against documents three and four of this section, evaluate the accuracy of this estimate in the number of Loyalists to be settled.

5) **"Estimate of the Lands that may be required to Settle the Disbanded and Refugee Loyalists in Canada"**

			Acres
	3 Field Officers	1000 ea.	3,000
1st & 2nd	18 Captains	700 ea.	12,600
Batn	47 Subalterns & Staff	500 ea.	23,500
K.R.R.N.Y.	120 Non Commissioned Officers	200 ea.	24,000
	842 Privates & Drummers	100 ea.	84,200
	700 (nearly) Women & Children	50 ea.	35,000
			182,300

Loyal Rangers	3 Field Officers	1000 ea.	3,000
	7 Captains	700 ea.	4,900
	24 Subalterns & Staff	500 ea.	12,000
	60 Non Commission Officers	200 ea.	12,000
	449 Privates & Drummers	100 ea.	44,900
	56 Gentlemen on Pensions &c.		22,800
	690 Women & Children	50 ea.	34,500
			134,100
Kings Rangers	1 Field Officer		1,000
	4 Captains	700 ea.	2,800
	5 Subalterns	500 ea.	2,500
	18 Non Commission Officers	200 ea.	3,600
	195 Privates	100 ea.	19,500
	206 Women & Children	50 ea.	10,300
			39,700
			356,100
Refugee Loyalists	2 Field Officers	1000 ea.	2,000
	10 Captains	700 ea.	7,000
	22 Subalterns	500 ea.	11,000
	257 Masters of Families	100 ea.	25,700
	1513 Single men, women & Children	50 ea.	75,650
	5251	Total	477,450
	21 Seigniorys at 23,040 ea.		483,840

Endorsed

P.A.C., Haldimand MSS., B169, pp. 121-122.

6) Report of John Collins and William Dummer Powell to Lord Dorchester on Loyalist Grievances

Kingston, 18th August 1787.

In Obedience to your Excellencys Instructions, We repaired to New Johnstown, now called Cornwall, and gave immediate Information to the Neighbourhood of the Object of our Mission. A few hours sufficed to Convince us that a very dangerous Jealousy and want of Confidence mutually subsisted in that Settlement, between the Majority of the settlers and their late Officers. . . .

. . . We plainly perceive that the People have been uniformly, and as if by System, kept ignorant of the exact extent of the bounty of Government to them – Secresy has been observed by the Officers and heads of Townships. We apprehend with a View only to sustain an appearance of Consequence and the Shadow of former power, but which with some Reason has excited the Jealousy of such among the people as were accustomed to reflection – This Jealousy has from various trifling Circumstances been gradually increasing untill the Certainty of some joint Communication with your Excellency and Ignorance of its purport inflamed their Suspicions into Rivalship and hatred. We are thoroughly convinced that if the Petition from the Heads of Townships to your Excellency had been communicated to the Inhabitants, before it was forwarded, your Lordship would not have heard a Murmer from these People on the Subject of a general Charge or Complaint against their Officers. . . .

P.A.C., R.G., 4, S28.

6.   The Hardships of the Loyalists

The hardships of the Loyalists are legendary. Examine most text-books and you will find great stress placed upon the difficulties faced by the Loyalists once they arrived in Upper Canada. A recently published book argues, however, that:

. . . these refugees experienced a kinder fate than have most exiles in the long sad tale of humanity uprooted. . . . They came to a new country but it was not a far country; sometimes they went back to their old homes to visit friends and relatives, and occasionally they even remained there. Much of the bitterness died down with the passing years, and it was not equally intense among all the Loyalists.[1]

The views of this secondary source may be examined in the light of the following primary sources.

1. Define the terms primary and secondary source.

2. What occupational background were most Loyalists suited to in Upper Canada?

3. Before reading the second document, make a list of articles which you, as a Loyalist, might request from the British government. Compare your list to that of the "Associated Loyalist" and account for any differences.

4. Do you agree or disagree with the quotation which introduces this section? Give reasons.

1) Memorial from Loyalists at Sorel

Sorel the 18th of January 1784.

His Excellency Lieutenant Genl. Frederick Haldimand Governor & Commander in Chief in and over His Majesty's Province of Quebec, &c. &c.

The Petition of the Subscribers Loyalists now residing at Sorel on behalf of themselves & others.

Most Humbly Sheweth

That the Petitioners previous to their Departure from New York for this Province were given to understand by His Excellency Sir Guy Carleton . . . should in every respect be put on same footing with other suffering Loyalists who had gone to Nova Scotia and that provisions and cloathing should be deliver'd at or shortly after our arrival in Canada to each Family as they stood on the Muster rolls made under the inspection of Persons appointed by the aforesaid Board for that purpose a day or two before our sailing; and that without any Discrimination of our respective Servants whether White or Black bound or free. These Provisions and cloathing for our Servants in particular

[1] G. M. Craig, *Upper Canada: The Formative Years, 1784-1791* (Toronto: McClelland and Stewart, Ltd., 1963), p. 7.

we Humbly Conceive His Excellency was pleased to promise from a knowledge of our great sufferings and losses sustained on account of our Loyalty and attachment to His Majesty & the British Constitution for which we have sacrificed our all; as well as to enable us the better to go through the Difficulties which he knew in forming a settlement in a strange Country.

With this promise we embarked for this place recommended to and looking up to your Excellency as our only benefactor in relieving our distresses and hearing our Complaint.

We therefore humbly beg leave to acquaint your Excellency That our poverty in our present situation is such as Exposes us to every inconvenience arising from the Inclemence of the present season for want of clothing, numbers of us having scarcely a whole Garment or a comfortable Blanket and find no hope of relief but from this application to your Excellency.

The Petitioners being thus in the greatest distress in a strange Country not within the reach of Relations who might administer Relief, nor one days Labour to be had at this Season for ourselves or Servants, Humbly pray your Excellency would be pleased to take their distressed situation into consideration by removing the cause of their present complaint which will prevent Numbers from suffering for want of Clothing. And the Petitioners as in duty bound will every pray.

P.A.C., Haldimand MSS., B138, pp. 331-334.

2) Memorial of the Associated Loyalists

To His Excellency Lieutenant General Haldimand Governor & Commander in Chief, &c., &c.

The request of the Companies of Associated Loyalists going to form a Settlement at Cataraque.

That Boards, Nails and Shingles be found each Family for Compleating such Buildings as they shall see Cause to Erect for their Convenience at any time for the space of Two years from & after their first Arrival at Cataraque with Eighty Squares of Window Glass to be delivered shortly after their arrival there.

That Arms & Ammunition with one Felling Ax be allowed for each Male Inhabitant of the age of fourteen years

One Plough shear & Coulter	One Gouge	
Leather for Horse Collers	Three Gimblets[1]	
Two Spades	One Hand Saw & Files	
Three Iron Wedges	One Nail Hammer	Be allowed
Fifteen Iron Harrow Teeth	One Drawing Knife	Each Family
Three Hoes	One Frow for splitting Shingles	
One Inch & half Inch Auger	Two Scythes & one Sickle	
Three Chisels (sorted)	One Broad Ax	

One Grind stone allowed for every Three Families.

One years Clothing to be issued to Each Family in proportion to their Numbers in the different species of Articles Issued to those gone to Nova Scotia.

[1] A small drill-like tool used to bore holes.

Two years Provisions to be found to Each Family in Proportion to their [Number] and Age.

Two Horses, Two Cows, and six Sheep to be delivered at Cataroque to Each Family at Government's Expence. The Cost of which to be made known at delivery To the End that the same may be a Moderate Tax, be again repaid to Government at the End of Ten Years if required – Our present Poverty & Inability to Purchase these Articles as well as our remote situation when there from Wealthy Inhabitants, will we hope pleed our Excuse in this respect.

That seeds of different kinds such as Wheat, Indian Corn, Pease, Oats, Potatoes & Flax seed be given to Each Family in quantity as His Excellency may think Proper.

That one Blacksmith be established in each Township & found with Tools & Iron for Two years at Government Expence for the use of the Inhabitants of each Town.

P.A.C., Haldimand MSS., B215, pp. 129-132.

3) From General Haldimand to Sir John Johnson

Quebec 14th June 1784.

Sir

I have at length the pleasure to acquaint you that I have received His Majesty's Instructions respecting the allowance of Provisions to be made to the Loyalists who settle upon Crown Lands in this Province, which is in every respect the same as in the Province of Nova Scotia, and is as follows – They are to be Victualled[1] at two thirds Allowance to the 1st of May 1785, and from that period at one third Allowance to the 1st day of May 1786, estimating the whole Return at one pound Flour, and one pound Beef, or Twelve ounces Pork; and the Children under Ten years to have a moiety[2] of the allowance made to grown Persons, it is directed that this Regulation shall take Place immediately. . . . . Altho' the present allowance falls short of that which I had ordered for them, yet considering that I had made it without authority, and the great uncertainty of its being continued, the Instructions are very satisfactory to me, and will I persuade myself, prove more beneficial to the Loyalists in the End, than the Years Allowance which I intended, if not prevented, to continue to them.

. . . , I have not the least authority to give them any further assistance. I trust to you to communicate this circumstance to the principal Persons amongst them, as well as to set them right in respect to discontents that have been encouraged by ill disposed Persons, as to prevent applications for relief which are daily made from all Quarters, and which, without the means of satisfying cannot but be very painful to me.

P.A.C., Haldimand MSS., B63, pp. 401-402.

[1] provided with food
[2] a half

4) Distribution of Clothing to the Refugee Loyalists as Approved by General Haldimand

Sorel 22nd May 1784.

Each Man and Boy above Ten Years of Age	Coats	1
	Waistcoats	1
	Breeches	1 Pair
	Hat	1
	Shirts (or 3½ yards Linen)	1
	Blankets	1
	Shoe Soles	1 Pair
	Leggings	1 Pair
	Stockings	1 Pair
Women or Girls above Ten Years of Age	Woolen Cloth	2 Yards
	Linen	4 D°[1]
	Stockings	1 Pair
	Blanket	1 D°
	Shoe Soles	1 D°
Children Under Ten Years of Age	Woolen Cloth	1
	Linen	2 D°
	Blanket (between 2)	1
	Stockings	1 Pair
	Shoe Soles	1 D^c

N.B.   Camp Equipage Issued a Tent for every Five Persons with a Camp Kettle for each tent.

P.A.C., R.G.4, S28, p. 116.

5) Reminiscence of Mrs. White of Whites Mills Near Cobourg Upper Canada. Formerly Miss Catherine Crysler [Crysdale] of Sydney, Near Bell[e]ville. Aged 79

My father and Mother came from England, settled in the United States, in St. Lawrence upon a farm which they purchased there, planted some trees and were begin[n]ing to prosper, when the revolutionary War broke out in 1774. Hearing that sugar was made from Trees in Canada, and being thorough Loyalists, and not wishing to be mixed up with the Contest about to be carried on, we packed up our effects and came over to Canada, arrived at Sorel they staid some time, but a fire happening at the house we occupied, in which the Deed of our land in the United States.

Guy Carleton, Lord Dorchester granted them 800 acres of Land, with some Implement to clear away the Trees and settle on lands Called Sidney near Bell[e]ville.

The Country at that time, was a complete wilderness, but by energy and perseverance, and a long time we got on very happily. . . .

[1] Ditto

In those secluded wilds, their trust was in Providence who blessed their endeavours.

They had two sons and five daughters; one of the boys was drowned.

Mother used to help to chop down the Trees, attended the house hold duties and as the children grew up, they were trained to Industrious habits, we were very useful to her, attended the cattle, churned the butter, making cheese, dressing the flax, spinning, in those days the spinning Wheel looked cheerful, made our own cloth, and stockings. I have a gown now in my possession that I made of home spun 60 years ago. We had no neighbours but an old Englishman who lived at some distance off who was an occasional visitor. Before our crops came round, having brought seed with us, supplied by Government, we had rations from the Military posts, also when these were nearly exhausted, father collected our Butter Cheese and spinning, taking them in a Batteaux to Kingston, which he traded off for salt, Tea, and flour – We had no Grist Mill at that time nearer than Kingston. The first Mill was put up at Napanee, afterwards.

The Bay of Quinte was covered with Ducks of which we could obtain any quantity from the Indians. As to fish they could be had by fishing with a scoup. I have often speared large Salmon with a pitchfork. Now and then provisions ran very scant, but there being plenty of Bull frogs we fared sumptuously. This was the time of the famine I think in 1788, we were obliged [to] dig up our potatoes after planting them to eat.

We never thought of these privations but were alway happy and cheerful, No unsettled minds no political strife, About Church Government or squabbling Municipal Councils. We left everything to our faithful Governor. I have often heard My father and Mother say, that they had no cause of complaint in any shape, and were always thankful to the Government for their kind assistance in the hour of need. Of an evening My father would make shoes of deer skins for the Children and Mother home spun dresses.

We had no Doctors, no Lawyers, No stated Clergy, we had prayers at home and put our trust in Providence. An old woman in the next clearing was the Chief Phys[i]cian to the surrounding Country as it gradually settled.

A tree fell one day and hurt Mother's back very much, we sent for the old woman who came steeped some wheat made lye, applied it very hot in a flannel, in a very short time, she was well as ever.

Flax was cultivated in those halcyon days. One year we grew 700 cwt.[1] We spun and wove it into table linin – wearing apparel. It lasted a very long time. A handy fellow came along and made us our Chamber looms, so that we could work away – and had no occasion for imported finery, nor if we had, we could not have procured any. As the girls grew up and settlers came round, a wedding occasionally took place.

There was but one Minister a Presbyterian, named Robert McDonall [McDowall] a kind warm hearted man who came on horse back through the woods from Kingston and where he saw smoke from a house he alway made up to the residence, where he was always welcome, he had a most powerful

[1] hundred weight

voice when he became excited, he could be heard a mile off.

All who were inclined to marry, he spliced, with many a kind word to the young folks, to be sure to be prosperous by industry and perseverance. He married Mr. White and myself I have the Certificate yet.

When the other girls would smirk and look so pleasant at him, think he was a great benefactor to the race for he would chuck them under the Chin and say, it will soon be your turn. I am going to Clark, a long way off through the Woods, with very few settlements on the way, and when I come back, mind and be ready.

There was not much trouble in that for the girls had no dresses but what they spun and made for themselves. We got along first rate so that when any of the girls married afterwards they each had a portion of a 100 acres 1 Cost 4 cows a yoke of steers 20 sheep and linin which they had spun and wove, some furniture which they made suited to their Log House.

Carpets were not known then, nor were they wanted, as the floors of a farm house were always scoured by their own industry.

Ontario Historical Society, Vol. X (Toronto, 1906), pp. 153-157.

6) Reminiscence of James Dittrick

The most trying period of our lives, was the year 1788 called the year of scarcity – everything at that period seemed to conspire against the hardy and industrious settlers.

All the crops failed, as the earth had temporarily ceased to yield its increase, either for man or beast – for several days we were without food, except the various roots that we procured and boiled down to nourish us. We noticed what roots the pigs eat; and by that means avoided anything that had any poisonous qualities. The officers in command at the military stations did all in their power to mitigate the general distress, but the supplies were very limited, consequently only a small pittance was dealt out to each petitioner.

We obtained something and were on allowance until affairs assumed a more favorable aspect. Our poor dog was killed to allay the pangs of hunger, the very idea brought on sickness to some, but other devoured the flesh quite ravenous. . . . We next killed a horse which lasted us a long time and proved very profitable eating; those poor animals were a serious loss to our farming appendages, but there was no help for it. . . .

At length a brighter era dawned upon us, and since then, everything went on well and prospered.

Public Archives of Ontario, 1860.

7.   The Forgotten Loyalists:

**The Six Nations
in the Late Eighteenth Century**

The Canadian public is today being made increasingly aware of
the appalling conditions under which Indian families must live.
Statistics have been published which reveal the life expectancy
of Indian women to be thirty-four years and that of men, thirty-
three years. Forty-seven per cent of Canadian Indian families
earn less than one thousand dollars a year, while forty per cent
live on welfare, and only forty-four per cent have electricity.[1]

While the statistics are disputable, the fact remains that the
Indians are the forgotten people of Canada. Most of our history
texts and courses, for example, have done very little to reveal
their role in Canadian or Ontario history. Yet, as C. M. Johnston
has written, "The dusky exiles from the Finger Lakes, the rem-
nants of those proud people who had long collaborated with the
Europeans who controlled the Hudson Valley, had shared defeat
and humiliation with their British allies on the battlefields of
New York."[2] Led by the Mohawk, Joseph Brant, the Six Nations'
Confederacy turned to the 'Great White Father' in Britain for
assistance. In the following sources the role played by the Six
Nations' Confederacy in the Loyalist migration is examined.

1. Who are the leaders? How are they chosen? What qualities do they
   posses?

2. What are the values cherished by Iroquoian society?

3. Compare these values to those in the eighteenth century England.

1) Iroquoian Government

... the governmt of [these Tribes] is very simple; the power is invested in the
Chiefs when assembled, they meet at the Council Fire, as they call it, because
they generally stand near a very comfortable one; here they discuss the various
subjects of importance which are brought before them & some deliver very
good sensible speeches; they generally begin by some compliment to the last
speaker, such as for instance they have listened attentively to words which
he has uttered & maturely considered them that they are persuaded that they
proceed from a sincere heart & desire for promoting the welfare of the 5 Nations;
any sentence calling forth the glory of the nations or their antiquity is always
well received & especially as they frequently use brethren of the same nation,
friends to the same country, & similar expressions, they are always sure to

[1] According to the National Indian Brotherhood.
[2] C. M. Johnston, *Brant County: A History 1784-1945* (Toronto:
Oxford University Press, 1967), p. 4.

obtain a favourable audience ... Mr. Norton[1] ... observed that another advantage attended these expessions; that they were of admirable Service when a man was at a loss: I think that this proves they are not wholy unacquainted with the art of Rhetoric. It is very remarkable that the Women are admitted to the Council fire & have the liberty of speaking, which is sometimes used; when the nature of the Education of this tribe is considered, the difference of the instruction of the girls & boys is so small, the sources of knowledge are so inconsiderable that I see no reason why a Woman with strong natural sense should not acquit herself in the Council with general Satisfaction. there are two kinds of Chieftains, the war Chief & the Civil Chief; the war Chief is wholy Elective any aimiable man remarkable for his bravery & courage, who has lived quietly & conducted himself with propriety is chosen a Chief – his good qualities render him eligible not his rank or possessions, the civil Chief is nearly hereditary; they are almost always chosen from particular families tho' not in what we should call ragular succession; sometimes a civil Chief are chosen a war Chief, & in this case supposing he has any talents for Oratory, he has the greatest influence where any one is making a speech he gives belts made of wamphum, to assist the memory in the different divisions of it a very great regard is paid for these belts; when the subject is of very great importance the belt is very wide & so on – If a Mohawk makes a promise to another, he gives him one of these belts – his word is irrevocable & they do not consider any thing a greater reproach then showing them the belts which they have distributed; here is your belt, this sentence is sufficiently binding – the traties[2] which they formerly made were oral & remembered by repeating them from Father to son. but the Memory is very much assisted by these Wampham belts When any Foreign Ambassador comes to them & makes any proposal they contrive to remember every word he says; different people are appointed to learn by heart a separate sentence & no more; so when they come to put it together they know every word of it ..., the five nations are remarkable for supporting each other in any distress; they have made treaties & Alliances for the purpose; their intermarriages in a general measure tend to strengthen them in this union – Mr. Norton mentioned a very beautiful Idea which they expressed, when danger from a foreign enemy was impending; that they should link the Chain of friendship in such a manner, that if any part was touched the whole should feel.

N.Y.S.L. (New York State Library) MSS. #13340-51.

1, Compare this source to Genesis in the Old Testament.

2. What moral values does this source reveal?

2) Iroquoian Mythology

... it's curious that they [Six Nations] always acknowledged an incomprehensible supreme being their Ideas concerning the formation & population

[1] John Norton (d. 1826), a Scot and friend of Joseph Brant was adopted by the Mohawks and studied their society intensively.
[2] Treaties

of the world are of this nature; it pleased the supreme to send from heaven,
or rather to let fall a pragnent Woman, she fell upon a large turtle which had
previously been prepared for her reception; the force of her fall occasioned
the turtle to move in some mud upon which he was lying & collected a considerable portion; the operation necessarily was slow nor was it to be compleated by
her alone: after a certin time a daughter was born; as soon as she was able
to work she helped her mother in the tedious work at which she laboured: she
increased in strength & beauty as she increased in years; one night however in
her sleep, the genius of the turtle came to her, and she should conceive two
sons that would be the destruction of their mother he placed by her side two
barbed arrows & departed. . . .

Accordingly she was with Child. before the children were born they began
to quarrel which should first & how they should come into the world, and also
in what manner; after much altercation they agreed to be born in the natural
manner provided that the good one, would appr. the first – The good one was
born; but the other disregarding his promise & agreement would come into the
world, through his mothers side – he did so and killed his Mother; he was on
this account called Taloiska or the bad principle or genious and his brother
Cateneuworga [?] or the good principle As they grew up they assisted their
grandmother in the formation of the world; which by this time had become of
a considerable size; Taloiska soon gave, instances of his bad disposition, which
his brother bore as well as he could. . . .

N.Y.S.L., MSS., #13350-51.

1. When compared to Europe, what does this source reveal about
   Indian society?

2. Compare the rôle of women in Iroquoian society to that of women
   in eighteenth century Britain.

3) The Influence of the Mohawk Women

. . . when they [the males] return from the hunting parties they deliver the
produce of their sport to the Women, whose property it exclusively is; indeed
every possession of the man Except his horse & his rifle belong to the Woman;
after Marriage: she takes care of their money & gives it to her husband as she
thinks his necessities require it . . . So different is this account given by Mr. Norton from the opinion generally entertained concerning the treatmt of the Women;
so far are they from being the slaves of their husbands, doing the hard labor
& resigning their property to him, as I have frequently heard asserted, the husband
has not the disposal of any part of it – Except what she chooses to give him. he
undertakes all laborious employments builds the house, repairs it, Cultivates
the soil procures food by hunting, & delivers to his Wife the produce of his
merchandize – this is a strong instance of the Erroneous opinions Entertained
concerning the Mohawks; they must have origenated in total ignorance of the
nation: as I do not know any one fact which can support them. . . . the truth is
that the Women are treated in a much more respectful manner then in England

& that they possess very superior power; this is to be attributed in a great measure to the system of their Education. . . .

N.Y.S.L., MSS., #13350-51.

1. What role did the Six Nations play in the war of the American Revolution?

4) Iroquoian War Tactics

I now come to a very important part of Mr. Nortons story what relates to the warfare of the 5 nations[1] – it is superfluous for me to say that a people who have been trained up in so hardy a manner & exercised so early in the use of arms should enter readily into war – indeed it is considered as the great opportunity for a man of courage to display his abilities; it is by no means unusual when two men quarrel, instead of engaging in a single combat as we are told the antients[2] did, or by fighting a duel as is more genteely the case at the present time, they proclaim what deeds they will perform in War & defy their antagonists to excel them – if there should happen to be any war at the time of the quarrel, they immediately join the army; . . . thus which ever of the two signalizes himself the most has the question in debate decided in his favor; like most nations which have not arrived at any great degree of civilization they practise what is called the war dance – . . . when properly performed Three or four stand near & sing a particular tune which is accompanied by the drums; then they get up in pairs & represent a battle; they first advance leaping from side to side with astonishing agility: this kind of zigzag motion is to prevent the adversary from taking a settled aim with his rifle; Mr. Norton says that this Maneuvre puzzles even the best shot; sometimes however they are hit when the combatants are come near to one another – they draw their swords & make a desperate Cut or two, one falls, the other takes out his knife, scalps his fallen adversary, hangs the scalp upon his girdle & retires exulting – I observed when Mr. Norton danced that his whole appearance was instantly changed – instead of being mild and humane, his countenance assumed a most savage & terrific look; he sprang forward to seize the enemy with amazing ferocity; the action was both manly and graceful . . . , they generally accompany all their songs with dancing – what I have already described is the war dance; it accompanies the war song; this Song in general contains & celebrates the exploits of the dancing hero . . . the Mohawks possesses very high and independent notions concerning peace and war; they are very tenacious of their rights & will fight on account of the least impringement of them when restitution is denied – If any of the tribes is injured it sends a remonstrance to the offending power – if it is not attended to, they send a second time, & soon a third time; & if they cannot by these means gain redress they wage war, the way in which they conduct a battle, is both singular & accellent[3]; when they come in sight of the enemy they advance each singing

---

[1] The sixth nation joined the Confederacy after the exodus to Canada.
[2] Ancients
[3] excellent

his war song they are made in general extempure[1]; they most commonly signify what they have before done against the people whom they are going to attack, or what they intend to do or what number of scalps they will bring away — when they have advanced far enough to use the rifle they proceed by divisions, so as always to keep up a constant fire — while one division advances & fires while the next is holding & so on — In general except upon very important cases they carry on a kind of desaltory[2] warfare which must be very distressing to an enemy; they go out in small parties, conceil[3] themselves under the bushes & when they see an opportunity of gaining any advantage, they Sally forth & are guided according to circumstances — there is a great advantage in this kind of attack; for an Enemy can never know how many may be concealed; thus it is right in a general to keep his men under arms when he seems but a very few of the opposite party — Mr. Norton mentioned a circumstance which shows a truth [?] of this remark, that 2 men and one boy hideing themselves and occasionally killing one or two kept the European troops under arms for two nights & a day — it is not uncommon upon any great occasion in a time of war, for the Women to follow the army to battle, shouting and incoraging them Mr. Norton said that in these cases the battle was always bloody, for when the Women could see the fight, every young man was anxious to show his courage & the Older warriors endeavoured to make the best use of their remaining activity — All this in case of victory was not prejudicial to them but it produced the most fatal consequences if the enemy gained any advantage; for Mr. Norton said then [when] the Ladies were not present, they persued the measured dictated by prudence & instead of maintaining a disadvantageous contest, would secure their safety by flight — but humanity compelled them, as Mr. Norton expressed, to expose their own lives for the purpose of letting the Women escape — . . . . the cruelty exercised by these tribes upon the prisoners taken in war has been a subject by many authors very fetile of polite Apostrophes[4] to the feelings of the human reader — the fact is that as a general rule the prisoners are adopted into the family of the Warrior who has taken thus the vacant place of a Grandfather or other relation that has lately died is filled up but so proud is the mortal spirit of some of these heros that when they are taken they enter into the enemies camp singing their war song telling what mischief they have done to them; how many they have killed and demand death, but I must observe that a good warrior is never taken unless surrounded so completely that he is no longer able to defend himself he prefers death to captivity —

N.Y.S.L. MSS. #13350-51.

1. What were the basic arguments in Brant's appeal to Haldimand?

2. Why did Haldimand feel it was so necessary to act quickly on the Indians' request?

[1] without preparation
[2] disconnected or random
[3] conceal
[4] exclamatory statement

3. What did the British government do to help the Indians? Was Britain motivated by kindness or necessity? Upon what principles did Britain base her Indian policy?

4. By examining the census taken in 1785 determine the groups which made up the six nations. What was the dominant group? Why?

5) The Six Nations' Exodus to the Grand Brant's[1] Speech to Haldimand at Quebec, May 21, 1783

Brother Asharekowa and Representatives of the King, the sachems[2] and War Chieftains of the Six United Nations of Indians and their Allies have heard that the King, their Father, has made peace with his children the Bostonians. The Indians distinguish by Bostonians, the Americans in Rebellion . . . and when they heard of it ,they found that they were forgot and no mention made of them in said Peace, wherefore they have now sent me to inform themselves before you of the real truth, whether it is so or not, that they are not partakers of that Peace with the King and the Bostonians.

Brother, listen with great attention to our words, we were greatly alarmed and cast down when we heard that news, and it occasions great discontent and surprise with our People; wherefore tell us the real truth from your heart, and we beg that the King will be put in mind by you and recollect what we have been when his people first saw us, and what we have since done for him and his subjects.

Brother, we, the Mohawks, were the first Indian Nation that took you by the hand like friends and brothers, and invited you to live amongst us, treating you with kindness upon your debarkation in small parties. The Oneidas, our neighbors, were equally well disposed towards you and as a mark of our sincerity and love towards you we fastened your ship to a great mountain at Onondaga, the Center of our Confederacy, the rest of the Five Nations approving of it. We were then a great people, conquering all Indian Nations round about us, and you in a manner but a handfull, after which you increased by degrees and we continued your friends and allies, joining you from time to time against your enemies, sacrificing numbers of our people and leaving their bones scattered in your enemies country. At last we assisted you in conquering all Canada, and then again, for joining you so firmly and faithfully, you renewed your assurances of protecting and defending ourselves, lands and possessions against any encroachment whatsoever, procuring for us the enjoyment of fair and plentiful trade of your people, and sat contented under the shade of the Tree of Peace, tasting the favour and friendship of a great Nation bound to us by Treaty, and able to protect us against all the world. . . .

It is as I tell you, Brother, and would be too tedious to repeat on this Pressing Occasion the many Proofs of Fidelity we have given the King our Father.

Wherefore Brother, I am now Sent in behalf of all the King's Indian Allies

[1] Joseph Brant, born on the Ohio River in 1742 and died at Burlington, Ontario in 1807, was the Six Nations' principal war chief and leader of migration to Upper Canada.
[2] chiefs

to receive a decisive answer from you, and to know whether they are included in the Treaty with the Americans, as faithful Allies should be or not, and whether those Lands which the Great Being above has pointed out for Our Ancestors, and their descendants, and Placed them there from the beginning and where the Bones of our forefathers are laid, is secure to them, or whether the Blood of their Grand Children is to be mingled with their Bones, thro' the means of Our Allies for whom we have often so freely Bled.

Colonial Office Papers (C.O.) 42, v. 44, pp. 133-135.

6) Haldimand to Sir John Johnson

Quebec, 26 May 1783.

. . . Since my last letter to you, I have conferred at large with Colonel Claus[1] and Joseph Brant upon the expediency of settling such of the Six Nations Indians on the North Side of Lake Ontario and River Niagara, as shall prefer that situation to the risk of returning to their former settlements, now subject to the Americans, and it gives me pleasure to find that Joseph so readily adopts the Plan. Uncertain when I shall receive Instructions from Home upon this interesting subject, and finding that the Indians are become very impatient of, and discontented with their present situation, and as I am informed by Joseph, they are in daily expectation of receiving proposals from the United States. . . . I wish you, without delay, to proceed to Niagara to quiet the apprehensions of the Indians by convincing them that it is not the Intention of Government to abandon them to the resentment of the Americans. Joseph will deliver to you my answer to the speech he brought in behalf of the Six Nations, which you will please communicate to them on your arrival at Niagara, with whatever speech may be proper from yourself upon the occasion.

P.A.C., Haldimand MSS., B115, 113.

7) Haldimand's Proclamation of October 25, 1784

Whereas His Majesty having been pleased to direct that in Consideration of the early Attachment to His Cause manifested by the Mohawk Indians, & of the Loss of their Settlement they thereby sustained that a Convenient Tract of Land under His Protection should be chosen as a Safe & Comfortable Retreat for them & others of the Six Nations who have either lost their Settlements within the Territory of the American States, or wish to retire from them to the British – I have, at the earnest Desire of many of these His Majesty's faithfull Allies purchased a Tract of Land, from the Indians situated between the Lakes Ontario, Erie & Huron and I do hereby in His Majesty's name authorize and permit the said Mohawk Nation, and such other of the Six Nation Indians as wish to settle in that Quarter to take Possession of, & Settle upon the Banks of the River commonly *called Ours* [Ouse] or Grand River, running into Lake Erie, allotting to them for that Purpose Six Miles deep from

[1] Daniel Claus (1727-1787) served as an Indian agent.

each Side of the River beginning at Lake Erie, & extending in that Proportion to the Head of the said River, which them & their Posterity are to enjoy for ever.

Given under my Hand & Seal &c &c
       25th Oct[r] 1784
(Signed) Fred: Haldimand

      P.A.C., Haldimand MSS., B222, 1061.

8) A Census of the Six Nations on the Grand River, 1785

	PERSONS
Mohawks	448
Onondagas Council fire	174
d° Bear's foot's party	51
Senecas	47
... Onondagas from the West	20
Upper Cayugas	198
Upper Tootalies [Tutelos]	55
Oghguagas[1]	113
Delaware Aaron's party	48
Oghguaga Joseph's party	49
Tuscaroras	129
Lower Cayugas	183
St. Regis	16
Montours	15
Creeks & Cherokees	53
Lower Tootalies	19
Delawares	183
Senecas from the West	31
Nanticokes	11
	1843

      P.A.C., Haldiman MSS., B103, 457.

9) "Means Suggested as the Most Probable to Retain the Six Nations and Western Indians in the King's Interest"

The Indians of the Six Nations, the Oneidas excepted, having taken an early, and a very sanguine part with Government have, by the Fate of the War, and Treaty of Peace, forfeited Their Country and many of them have been driven entirely out of it, with the loss of valuable Possessions. Seeing the Policy, as well as necessity of providing a Retreat for Them, I made a purchase of a Tract of Land for that purpose from the Chipawa & Mississiague Nations on the North side of Lake Ontario where numbers are now settling, having assisted them with Provisions & Implements for building and establishing Themselves, all which, I had the Honor, duly to report to Lord Sidney.

    [1] Mohicans

Upon my departure from Quebec I left directions to send the Engineer at Niagara to mark out their Towns &c. and to assist Them in building a Church and School-House, for which They expressed great anxiety – this Settlement should meet with every Indulgence and Encouragement of Government, not only in consideration of Their past Services, but in proportion as it shall be though necessary to preserve the Friendship & Alliance of the Indians in general, whose Conduct is always governed by that of the Six Nations, in other Words, *the Possession of the Upper Country and the Furr Trade*, and these Measures should be taken without delay that the Indians may be comfortably established and experience the Sweets of the King's Protection. . . .

A certain quantity of Presents will be indispensibly necessary, They should be puntually supplied, so as never to disappoint the Indians; but it is high time the the Expence attending these donations should be reduced to a narrow compass which, with a prudent management and distribution of the Presents may be done without alarming, or distressing the Indians. The Conduct of the Western Indians & Tribes depending (tho' infinitely a more numerous People) will always be influenced by that of the Six Nations . . . some Present and marks of Friendship are nevertheless due to Their past Services, and should be, from time to time, dispensed amongst Them. . . .

P.A.C., Haldimand MSS., B119, 322-324.

1. How would you evaluate the Indians' success in adjusting to their new environment?

2. What problems, stated or implied, might confront the Indians?

10) A Visit with Joseph Brant on the Grand River, 1792

. . . we . . . mounted our sleas, and drove on to the Indian village, alighted about nightfall all the house of the famous Indian chief and warrior, Captain Joseph Brant. This renowned warrior is not of any royal or conspicuous progenitors, but by his ability in war, and political conduct in peace, has raised himself to the highest dignity of his nation, and his alliance and friendship is now courted by sovereign and foreign states. Of this there are recent instances, as he has had within the last three weeks several private letters and public dispatches from Congress, soliciting his attendance at Philadelphia on matters of high importance; but after consulting Colonel Gordon, commandant of the British troops in this place, and all Upper Canada, he excused himself and declined to accept of the invitation. He just now enjoys a pension and captain's half pay, from the British government, and seems to keep quite staunch by it; but a person of his great political talents ought to be cautiously looked after; at the same time I am convinced he bears no good will to the American States, . . .

Captain Brant who is well acquainted with European manners, received us with much politeness and hospitality. Here we found two young married ladies, with their husbands, on a visit to the family, both of them very fair complexioned and well looking women. But when Mrs. Brant appeared

superbly dressed in the Indian fashion, the elegance of her person, grandeur
of her looks and deportment, her large mild black eyes, symmetry and
harmony of her expressive features, though much darker in the complexion,
so far surpassed them, as not to admit of the smallest comparison between
the Indian and the fair European ladies; I could not in her presence so much
as look at them without marking the difference Her blanket was made up of
silk, and the finest English cloth, bordered with a narrow stripe of embroidered
lace, her sort of jacket and scanty petticoat of the same stuff, which came down
only to her knees; her gaiters or leggans of the finest scarlet, fitted close as a
stocking, which showed to advantage her stout but remarkably well formed
limbs; her mogazines [Indian shoes] ornamented with sik ribbons and beads.
Her person about five feet nine or ten inches high, as streight and proportionable
as can be, but inclined to be jolly or lusty. She understands, but does not speak
English. I have often addressed her in that language, but she always answered
in the Indian tongue. . . .

Tea was on the table when we came in, served up in the handsomest China
plate and every other furniture in proportion. After tea was over, we were
entertained with the music of an elegant hand organ, on which a young Indian
gentleman and Mr. Clinch[1] played alternately. Supper was served up in the same
genteel stile. Our beverage, rum, brandy, Port and Madeira wines. Captain
Brant made several apologies for his not being able to sit up with us so long
as he wished, being a little out of order, and we being fatigued after our
journey went timeously[2] to rest; our beds, sheets, and English blankets, equally
fine and comfortable.

Next day being Sunday, we the visitors went to church. The service was
given out by an Indian in the absence of the minister, who was indisposed,
and I never saw more decorum or attention paid in any church in all my life.
The Indian squaws sung most charmingly, with a musical voice I think peculiar
to themselves. After sermon I went to the school house to converse with the
master, an old Yanky. As it was Sunday, the scholars were not convened, so
that I had not the pleasure of seeing them. He teaches English and arithmetic
only. He told me he had sixty-six on his list, some of whom had excellent
capacities for learning, and read distinctly and fluently. After this I visited
several houses in the village, and found the inhabitants had abundance of the
necessaries of life to supply their wants, and are better and more comfortably
lodged than the generality of the poor farmers in my country. Few of the houses
I saw but had two apartments, deal floors, and glass windows. They have a deal
of crop, and excellent cattle, inferior to none I have seen in the province. The
old people attend farming, while the young men range the woods for different
sorts of game, and supply the family with venison, of which they generally have
more than suffices; the overplus they sell to the white inhabitants in the neighbourhood. I have seen many loads of venison come in to the market of Niagara,
and it is rare to find in the season a house without some . . . I remarked of the
Indians in this part of the Continent, that they never speak in a hasty or rapid

[1] Ralph Clench (1762?-1828) served in Butler's Rangers, and was an
early resident of Niagara.
[2] timely

manner, but in a soft, musical, and harmonious voice. I am charmed with the mildness of their manners when friendly, but when enemies their ferocity has no bounds. Dinner was just going on the table in the same elegant stile as the preceding night, when I returned to Captain Brant's house, the servants dressed in their best apparel. Two slaves attended the table, the one in scarlet, the other in coloured clothes, with silver buckles in their shoes, and ruffles, and every other part of their apparel in proportion. We drank pretty freely after dinner, Port and Madeira wines, as already observed; but were not pressed to more than we chose. . . .

After dinner Captain Brant, that he might not be wanting in doing me the honours of his nation, directed all the young warriors to assemble in a certain large house, to show me the war dance, to which we all adjourned about night-fall. Such as were at home of the Indians appeared superbly dressed in their most showy apparel, glittering with silver, in all the variety, shapes, and forms, · of their fancies, which made a dazzling appearance; the pipe of peace with long white feathers, and that of war with red feathers, equally long, were exhibited in their first war dance, with shouts and war hoops resounding to the skies. The chief himself held the drum, beat time, and often joined in the song, with a certain cadence to which they kept time The variety of forms into which they put their bodies, and agility with which they changed from one strange posture to another, was really curious to an European eye not accustomed to such a sight. Several warlike dances were performed, which the chief was at particular pains to explain to me. . . .

With Captain Brant I had a conversation upon religion, introduced by him, indeed, and not by me. He said, that we were told every one that was not a Christian would go to hell; if so, what would become of the miserable souls of many Indians who never heard of Christ? asked if I believed so, and what I thought of it? I told him very frankly, that if all the saints and priests on earth were to tell me so, I would not believe them. With such as were instructed in the Christian religion, and did not conform to its precepts, I did not doubt but it would fare the worse; that I believed it might be so with those of every other religion; but that I supposed it was a matter of no moment in the omnipotent eye of the Creator of the universe, whether he was worshipped on Sundays in the church, or on Saturdays in the mosque; and that the grateful tribute of every one would be received, however different the mode of offering might be; that every man has only to account for those actions which he knew to be wrong at the time of committing them; but for these, that surely a time of reckoning would come. He spoke of the Virgin Mary, and her husband Joseph, and even of our Saviour, in a way that induced me to wave the subject. It however showed the difficulty of converting these people from the early prejudice of education; . . .

. . . But before I take leave of this charming country, and the honours done by this renowned chief, and his warlike tribe of handsome young warriors, all of the Mohawke nation, I must not omit saying, that it appears to me to be the finest country I have as yet seen; and by every information I have had, none are more so in all America. The plains are very extensive, with a few trees here and there interspersed, and so thinly scattered as not to require any clearing, and hardly sufficient for the necessaries of the farmer; – the soil rich, and a deep clay mold. The river is about 100 yards broad, and navigable for large battoes to Lake Erie, a space of sixty miles, excepting for about two miles of what is called here rapids, but in Scotland would be termed fords, and in which the battoes are easily poled up against any little stream there may be. Abundance of fish are caught here in certain seasons, particularly in spring; such as Sturgeon, Pike, Pickerel, . . . and others peculiar to this country; and the woods abound with game. The habitations of the Indians are pretty close on each side of the river as far as I could see, with a very few white people interspersed among them, married to squaws and other of half blood, their offspring. The church in the village is elegant, the school house commodious, both built by the British government, who annually order a great many presents to be distributed among the natives; ammunition and warlike stores of all the necessary kinds; saddles, bridles, kettles, cloth, blankets, tomahawks, with tobacco pipes in the end of them; other things, and trinkets innumerable, provisions and stores; so that they may live, and really be, as the saying is, as happy as the day is long. . . .

I called at different villages or castles, as they are called here, and saw the inhabitants have large quantities of Indian corn in every house a-drying, and suspended in the roofs, and every corner of them. We put up at the house of a Mr Ellis, who treated us very hospitably. . . .

> P. Campbell, *Travels in the Interior Parts of North America in the Years 1791 and 1792* (Edinburgh: 1793), pp. 188-211.

Topics for Further Inquiry

1. Part One has attempted to introduce the historical process. Describe this process by applying knowledge gained from the readings.

2. Was Joseph Brant a genuine Canadian hero or self-seeking opportunist?

3. By examining the historical background of your local community, discover the origins of its founders, their reasons for settling where they did, and how their values and attitudes have affected your community to date?

4. "The winter seemed colder that year. Perhaps the loss of home, possessions and loved ones made it seem that way. We treked endlessly northward, mile after arduous mile, heading for Sorel and the protection of His Majesty's Government."

   Using this as an introductory sentence, construct an historical fiction based on the Loyalists in Upper Canada.

5. Based upon your study of Part One, write an 800 to 1000 word essay entitled *The Life and Times of a Typical Loyalist*.

TWO

A Pioneer Community
c. 1791-1812

The Loyalists provided Britain with more problems than those of the settlement and provisioning of a destitute people. The "Mother Country" now faced the dilemma which confronts Canada today, that of governing people of different races, religions, and languages. Pressured by the Loyalists who objected to landholding based on the French seigneurial system, a civil law administered on the French pattern and an unrepresentative government, Britain passed the Constitutional Act in 1791. It separated Upper and Lower Canada, provided for a representative government, and established landholding and legal practice based on the British example.

The following readings provide an opportunity to study Upper Canada in its formative years, for it was these years which stamped the province with its unique character. You will discover how Upper Canadians made a living, organized their society, worshipped, educated their children and governed themselves.

1.   An Infant Economy

Part One concluded that most Loyalists in Upper Canada were farmers, and their needs, based on available sources, were land, food and basic tools for farming. From the following source, determine the progress of Upper Canadian farmers since the dark days of the early 1780's when the Loyalists first arrived.

1. What were the values of Upper Canadian rural society?

2. What problems did an Upper Canadian farmer have to face?

3. What natural advantages did he enjoy? How did he get the capital (land, tools, etc.) to make a start? What help did he have to develop his farm? Why were large families an economic advantage? Why did the wages for labourers increase at harvest time?

4. What factors determined the prices and produce of the Upper Canadian farmer?

5. What similarities and differences exist between the Upper Canadian agricultural system and present day methods?

1) La Rouchefoucault[1] Describes the State of Upper Canadian Agriculture

The process of clearing woodlands is here the same, as all over America. The husbandmen harrow the cleared ground two, three, or four years successively; during which time wheat is sown. Then they plough, but in a very imperfect manner, and sow pease or oats, and again wheat, and so on, according to the common routine. The land yields, in this state, from twenty to thirty bushels per acre.

Corn, for the winter, is sown from the beginning of August till the end of September. Snow falls generally in the latter days of November, and remains on the ground until the beginning of April. Under this cover the blade gets up remarkably well, the corn ripens in July, and the harvest begins about the end of that month. For want of reapers, the scythe is made use of, which causes a great waste of corn, that cannot be housed, and merely serves for feeding pigs. Labourers, whose common wages are from three to four shillings (Halifax currency), are paid during the harvest at the rate of one dollar, or six shillings a day. Some farmers hire Canadians for two or three months, to whom they pay seven or eight dollars per month, and find them in victuals. It frequently happens, that these Canadians, who bind themselves by a written contract, meet with people offering them more money than they receive from their masters, which not being allowed to accept, they, of course, grow dissatisfied, and work negligently. They must be procured from the environs of Montreal. Farmers, who have no acquaintance in that country, find it difficult to obtain them; . . . The harvest work is therefore generally performed by the family: thus the housing of the crops, though it proceed slowly, is yet accomplished; . . . The soil, which is but of a middling quality in the vicinity of the town, is excellent about the bay; many farmers possess there to the number of one hundred and fifty acres of land, thoroughly cleared.

The climate of America, especially that of Canada, encourages the imprudence and covetousness of the farmers. There is no danger here, as in Europe, of the hay rotting, and the grain being spoiled by rains, if not speedily housed. There seldom passes a day without sunshine; the sky is seldom entirely overcast, it never rains but during thunder-storms, and this rain never continues longer than two hours. Grain is, besides, seldom liable here to blights, or any other kind of disease.

The cattle are not subject to contagious distempers; they are numerous without being remarkably fine. The finest oxen are procured from Connecticut, at the price of seventy or eighty dollars a yoke. Cows are brought either from the state of New York, and these are the finest; or from Canada: the former

[1] La Rouchefoucault-Liancourt was a French noble forced into exile by the French Revolution.

cost twenty, and the latter fifteen dollars. These are small in size, but, in the opinion of the farmers, better milch-cows, and are for this reason preferred. There are no fine bulls in the country; and the generality of farmers are not sensible of the advantages to be derived from cattle of a fine breed. In summer the cattle are turned into the woods; in winter, that is, six months together, they are fed on dry fodder, namely, with the straw of wheat, rye, or pease, and on most farms with hay cut on swampy ground, but by rich and prudent farmers with good hay. . . . There is no ready market at which a farmer can sell that part of his cheese and butter, which is not wanted for the use of his family. Of cheese and butter, therefore, no more is made, than the family need for their own consumption. They generally begin in the first days of May to make a provision for the winter. Some few farmers manufacture coarse woollens for their own clothing; the more usual way, however, is to buy the clothes. The farmer is too busy, has too little assistance, and makes his calculations with two little judgment, to engage in such a multiplicity of labours.

Sheep are more numerous here than in any part of the United States, which we have hitherto traversed. They are either procured from Lower Canada or the state of New York, and cost three dollars a head. They thrive in this country, but are high legged, and of a very indifferent shape. Coarse wool, when cleaned, costs two shillings a pound. There are few or no wolves, rattle-snakes, or other noxious animals, in this country.

The price of wheat is one dollar per bushel; last year the price was much lower; but it has risen from the general failure of the harvest. Fire-wood, delivered in the town, costs one dollar a cord; in winter it is conveyed thither in sledges from all the islands and banks of the river, which are covered with wood.

The river freezes over at the distance of twenty miles above Kingston.

The price of land is from two shillings and six-pence to one dollar per acre, if the twentieth part be cleared. This price rises in proportion to the number of acres cleared of wood, though influenced by occasional circumstances. Two hundred acres, one hundred and fifty of which were cleared, were very lately sold for one thousand six hundred dollars. The expence for cutting down all the large trees on an acre, and inclosing it with a fence as rude as in the United States, amounts to eight dollars.

There is no regular market in Kingston; every one provides himself with fresh meat as well as he can, but frequently it cannot be had on any terms.

W. R. Riddell, ed., *La Rochefoucault-Liancourt's Travels in Canada*, 1795 (Ontario Bureau of Archives, Thirteenth Report, 1916), pp. **71-75.**

2.   Commercial Activity

Not all Upper Canadians became farmers. Some, like Richard Cartwright, mentioned in Part One, took up the life of a colonial merchant. The following six sources, taken from Cartwright's papers, not only give insight into the life of a successful Upper Canadian merchant, but also reveal a great deal about the economy of the entire province.

1. From the first two selections, describe the ways in which trade was carried on. What products did Upper Canada produce? What markets did the province have for its produce? What factors affected the price which Upper Canadians received for their products? How did Britain aid this infant economy?

2. What problems did Upper Canadian merchants face?

3. What industry must have existed in Upper Canada in order to export the products stated by Cartwright? What practical problem was resolved by turning wheat into whiskey?

1) From Richard Cartwright to Davison & Co.
London, 4th Nov. 1797

Not having a seaport in our Province, it would be impossible or extremely inconvenient for any person here to import goods except through the medium of a Montreal house. Goods must be there received, the damages they have sustained at sea (as this sometimes happen) looked into and authenticated; from thence they must be carted to Lachine, where boats and men are to be procured to transport them this far. On the other hand, payments can be made there in bills or money when it would be difficult to convert them into remittances for England. Furs must be there examined, sorted and baled; potash[1] inspected, and lumber culled.[2] The mode usually practised here is this: the merchant sends his order for English goods to his correspondent at Montreal, who imports them from London, guarantees the payment of them there, and receives and forwards them to this country for a commission of five per cent on the amount of the English invoice. The payments are all made by the Upper Canada merchant in Montreal, and there is no direct communication whatever between him and the shipper in London. The order, too, must be limited to dry goods, and he must purchase his liquors on the best terms he can in the home market; and if he wishes to have his furs or potash shipped for the London market, he pays a commission of one per cent on their estimated value; if sold in Montreal, he is charged two and one-half per cent on the amount of the sales.

     C. E. Cartwright, *op. cit.*, pp. 76-77.

[1] Potash was obtained from wood ashes. It was useful in making soap and fertilizer.
[2] selected

2) From Richard Cartwright to J. G. Simcoe, Kingston, 15th Decr. 1794

Sir:

In the Account herewith enclosed your Excellency will see at one view the Quantity and Value of such Part of our last years surplus Produce as hath been either exported or furnished on the Spot for the use of Government. To this may be added about four thousand five hundred Bushels of wheat & other Grain consumed within the year by our Breweries & Distilleries, and which otherwise must have been exported in Exchange for a much smaller portion of Spirits and malt liquor than it has produced on the Spot; and may be considered as having added at least the Amt of the freight of the Corn to Montreal, and of the Beer & Spirits from thence as well as the value of the Casks to the Capital Stock of the Districts, or to use a language more conformable to our Circumstances, as having us to expend so much more for Cloathing & other Articles.

I find also upon very particular Inquiry, that the quantity of Pork collected here this Fall exceeds eight hundred Barrels. This is more by nearly three fourths than was produced last year, and it would have been still more considerable if the very great Drought of the last summer had not almost destroyed the Crops of Indian Corn on which the Pork in this Country is usually fattened. If no similar misfortune should occur, I expect in the Course of next Autumn twelve hundred Barrels may be collected here. . . .

I am sorry to observe that our prospects for Wheat & Flour are not equally favorable; for although from the best information that I can collect, we have about five thousand Bushels of Wheat on hand of the Crop of 1793, yet I think it doubtful whether we shall be able to do more than meet the internal demands for this Article, including the necessary supplies for the Troops, and the appearance of that destructive Insect; the Hessian Fly[1] amongst us has occasioned great anxiety about this important branch of our Agriculture.

It is a more pleasing Circumstance to call to your Excellency's Notice, that while the Agriculture of the Country is greatly encouraged by supplying the different Articles of Provision wanted for the Troops as far as possible from the Province, a very considerable Expense is thereby saved to Government, . . .

The Article of Potash, included among our Exports, is very much on the decline; owing in part to the rise of freight and Insurance and the reduction of price in England occasioned by the War; but principally to the high price of labour in the Country, and the difficulty of procuring Hands at almost any price.

Considerable quantities of Staves & even Masts & Spars[2] have been sent from this District since the year 1784; but this business hath within this year or two been altogether abandoned here – In the Eastern District however it

[1] A fly, of which the larva is destructive to wheat, so named because it was erroneously supposed to have come to America with troops from the German province of Hesse during the war of Independence.
[2] Pole for extending the sails of a ship.

is still carried on, though to no very great extent, in the Article of Boards & Staves, and greater quantities of Potash are also manufactured there than in this District. . . .

These Observations as connected with the Subject of the enclosed Paper are most respectfully submitted to your Excellency, by

Your Excellency's most obedient Servt.
Richard Cartwright.

E. A. Cruikshank, ed., *The Correspondence of Lieutenant Governor John Graves Simcoe* (Toronto: Ontario Historical Society, 1923-1931), IV, pp. 221-222.

Using information given in the following two documents:

4. compare the products exported (down) from Upper Canada in 1786 with those in 1794. Note any significant differences. What conclusions can be drawn?

5. Define the terms import (up) and export (down). Why was flour an import in 1786 and an export in 1794?

6. To what extent do these sources reveal Upper Canada's products, its markets, and its dependence on Britain?

3) Goods Handled by Hamilton and Cartwright at Cataraqui or Carleton Island,[1] 1786

Up   Tobacco, Tea, Paper, Sealing Wax, Flour, Indian goods, Rum, Black Strap, Russian Sheeting, Strouds[2], Blankets, Powder & Shott, White & green Molton[3], Ratteen[4], Scarlet Cloth, Floured Gatering, Silver Works – Broaches, Arm Bands, Crosses, Cheese, Handkerchiefs, Sugar, Liquor, Salt, Quills, Sickles, Coarse Cloth.

Down   Pearl Ash, Pot Ash, Deer Skins, Ginseng[5], Corn, Peas.

Pelteries – Beaver plt 7/6, Otters, good 20/–, Fishers 4/6, Martins 3/4, Minks 2/–, Raccoons 1/9, Bears 16/–, Cubbs 8/–, Foxes 3/–, Loups Lavee[6] 10/–, Carcajoux[7] 12/–, Muskrats 6, Deerskins 2/6, Castors 6/8.

P.A.O. *Cartwright Letter Book*, MS. 43.

[1] Carleton Island, near Kingston was used as a military post and transshipment point.
[2] Material from which blankets were made.
[3] A type of cloth?
[4] A thick woollen cloth.
[5] A root used to manufacture a medicine.
[6] Probably means washed wolf skins.
[7] American badgers.

4) **Account of Wheat, Flour & Other Articles the Produce of
the Midland District of Upper Canada, Exported from
the Town of Kingston, or Delivered there for the use of His
Majesty's Troops during the year 1794, with their value, ...**

EXPORTED TO LOWER CANADA

12823	Bus.[1] Wheat, Winchester Measure at	3/	£ 1923.9.–
896	Barls[2] of Flour	23/4	1045.6.8
83	do. of Midlings or Biscuit Flour	15/	62.5.–
3016	lbs. Hogs lard.	6d	75.8.–
15	tons Potash.	£18.	270.–.–
			£ 3376.8.8.

FURNISHED FOR THE USE OF THE TROOPS

3240	Bbls.[3] of Flour	23/4.	£ 3780.–.–
2938	Bus. of Peas	4/6	661.1.
480	Barls of Pork	90/	2160.
			£ 6601.1.

EXPORTED TO NIAGARA & YORK

1624	Bus. Wheat	3/	£ 243.12.
356	Bbls. Flour	23/4	415.6.8.
2500	lbs. Gammon[4]	8d.	83.6.8.
			£ 742.5.4.

RECAPITULATION

Amt. of Articles exported to L. Canada	£ 3376.8.8.
do. furnished for the use of the Troops	6601.1.
do. exported to Niagara & York	742.5.4.
Total Curry at 5/ the dollar	£10719.15.

Richard Cartwright.

Cruickshank, *The Simcoe Papers, op. cit.,* IV, p. 223.

---

7. What problems of transportation did Cartwright identify in the first
document? What further transportation difficulties do these following sources identify? How would such problems affect the price of
articles bought from Upper Canadian merchants?

[1] bushel.
[2] barrel.
[3] Barrels.
[4] Smoked or cured hams (bacon).

5) Cartwright to Messrs McTavish & Frobisher,[1] Kingston, 21 Aug, 1795

... In Boat No 16 one of the Kegs high wines was found to have been tapped under the hoops & wanted 1½ Q^{s2} of being full. It is a pity some example could not be made to deter the men from such practices for though they are sometimes detected yet they are so dextrous at these tricks that they frequently elude our utmost vigiliance. . . .

PAO, Cartwright Letter Book, MS. 43.

6) Cartwright to Messrs. Jas & A. McGill & Co., Kingston, 21 July, 1802

I arrived here yesterday & have yet had hardly had Time to look about me but I find that the Greater part of my English Goods have come to hand & that Mr Robison[3] has forwarded Pot Ash & Flour as they have come to hand & as Opportunities have offered. I am sorry for the Disaster that befel my first Scow, & as so many have since gone down safely I am inclined in some measure to impute it to the Ignorance or Want of Attention in the Pilot; and I doubt not that you will so care for the Flour as to make the Damage fall as lightly as possible. . . .

Ibid., MS. 44, p. 111.

7) Despard[4] to Quetton St. George,[5] July 23d. 1810

I am sorry to Inform you that last Wednesday I Received letters by Capt. Monger from Montreal, mentioning that the Ship John from Liverpool Bound for Montreal with all your woolens, and a Number, for others, was taken by a French Privateer – this circumstance I suppose will oblige you to go Down to Montreal Sooner than you intended in order to replace the loss, as Cloths are very plenty in Montreal, and the sooner as was there the better bargain could be got. . . .

Toronto Public Library, St. George Papers II.

8) Wood[6] to Leslie, McNaught & Co.,[7] U. Canada, York, 25th. October, 1808

... if a little more attention is paid in marking, packing and shipping Goods and if shipped in a vessel direct for Montreal would save the packages much ill usage they receive in unloading two or three times, however as it is an

[1] Merchants in Montreal.
[2] quarts
[3] A merchant at Niagara.
[4] Merchant at Niagara.
[5] A prominent merchant at York, later called Toronto.
[6] Alexander Wood, a merchant at York.
[7] A firm of suppliers in Glasgow, Scotland.

advantage to have them early as possible, probably the first Ships do not clear out for Montreal but were the same attention paid to the packing & packages marks &c as in London they might be reshipped fifty times without suffering in the least – I also complained of some of the articles and repeat the Complaint the hardware Knives and forks the large Kind Hinges locks &c are the veriest trash that ever workman put out of his hands – for the credit of my country I would wish they had been from any other place. On the Sugar I shall not be able to make up the expenses and duty, the quantity is about three times as much as ordered, and the Quality indifferent badly packed and in every day a disgrace to those who manufactured papered and patched up. On the other hand the Cloths Blankets Callicos &c. were exceedingly well packed came in good order and are excellent goods the looking Glasses are not such as I ordered and came each at the price of a Doz. of the Kind wanted, they will remain a dead Stock on my hands, one of the Cases of hats was so chattered that the Rats had got in and destroyed half the Contents. I before certified the articles short sent to wit 2 pair Japand bed Room Candlesticks, . . . and some triffling thing of Crockery – but on this last articles one Doz. Qt. Queens ware sent more than charged which made up the wastage on that article. . . .

T.P.L., Alexander Wood Letter Book, p. 218.

8. Since Upper Canada had no currency of its own, determine how commerce was carried on. What were the disadvantages of Upper Canada's lack of common currency?

9. List problems that might result in our own society if we did not have a common currency.

10. By referring back to the first document, suggest why Cartwright prefers to take "the Risque" referred to in document ten?

9) Advertising in Early Upper Canada

Mr. Q. St. George begs leave to inform his Friends and Customers that he has arrived from Montreal, and brought with him an ample stock of FALL & WINTER GOODS, also Crockery, Glass Ware, Cutlery and Ironmongery, and a handsome and well chosen assortment of Furriery; having arranged with a respectable Furrier there, all orders for articles in that line, from his friends here, will be forwarded by him, and their execution immediately attended to. He has also received from New-York a variety of Beaver Bonnets, of the newest fashions, and a general assortment of Millinery, among which are elegant and the most fashionable Ostrich Feathers, &c. &c. The length of time he devoted at Montreal to the purchase and selection, has enabled him to lay in his goods, this year, on the most favorable terms, and he can supply Country Store-keepers more advantageously to them than if they made their purchases below – He proposes to receive in payment and barter for Goods, the following articles, so soon as his stores will be fitted for their reception, viz: – Flour, Wheat, Indian Corn, Oats, Pease and Pork. None of these articles will be received unless they are of prime qualities, and he hopes none other will be offered; the Pork must be well cured and packed in sufficient barrels, and warranted for twelve months; the barrel marked with the venders name, and date of delivery.

Cash advanced as usual on account of Sterling Bills[1], which he will receive in payment from his regular Customers at par, although subject to a large discount in other places. He flatters himself that his Country-Friends and Customers, witnessing his exertions, will, by more regular payments in future, enable to continue them, to their mutual convenience and advantage. . . .

York Gazette, November 11, 1807.

10) **Cartwright's financial arrangements**

Inclosed you will find a bill of Exchange J. Elmsley on the Revd P. Elmsley for 786 Stlg.[1] also Capt. J. W. Miers, Lieutenant Churches & Ensign Crawfords Half Pay[2] which please to pass to the Credit of my Acct.[3] With Respect to the 354 Bbls shipped for England I will prefer taking the Risque of them myself to accepting 20 Stlg p[4] Bbl at Montreal & paying of Charges. –

PAO, Cartwright Letter Book, MS. 44, p. 111.

11. What problems could have resulted from the financial dealings described in documents eleven and twelve? What were the consequences of extreme indebtedness?

11) **Timothy Nightingale to Quetton St. George, Whitby May 28 1808**

As Anderson has disappointed me about taking my farm I am like to disappoint you about the Money due you it is out of my power to pay you unless I sell my farm which if for Sale I have offered to sell for three or four hundred Dollars less then the Value of it but if you know any body that will buy it please to send them and I will take the same that Anderson was to give in order that you may get your pay or I will let you have half of it for twelve Shillings an Acre which is worth Double what I offer it to you for or I will deliver my farm to you and you may let it out till you get your pay I cant offer anything more if I cant sell and you wont Comply with these terms to gaol I must go. . . .

NB   You need not send no officer any more only send a line and I will come up immediately and go to gaol if you say so . . .

P.A.O., Baldwin Papers.

[1] Sterling Bills were the equivalent of English pound (240 Pence).
[2] Government pension to former military men.
[3] Account
[4] Silver, of which originally a pound came to have a standard purchase value.

12) **Nightingale to Quetton St. George, Whitby July 22 1808**

I have ben atrying to get the money for you to pay you which you know that twice I have ben disopinted I am agoing to make potash to see if I cant pay you that way if you will Let me alone till I can turn my self to make it part this fall and part in the Spring I shall do my best to pay you I will pay you the Interest of the money from this date you draw no Interest after Judment but if you will wate I am willing to pay Interest if you put me to gail I cant be in the way to pay you then but to spend what I have and then sarten you wont get your pay from your humble sarvent

Ibid.

---

12. Based on the previous sources as well as the following selections, indicate how Upper Canada's colonial relationship to Britain affected her commerce.

13) Upper Canada pays no taxes, except a duty on wine, amounting to four-pence per gallon on Madeira, and two-pence on other sorts of wine, and another of thirty-six shillings sterling a year for a tavern-licence, which, during the session of 1793, was encreased by twenty shillings Canada currency[1]. The sum total of the public revenue amounts to nine hundred pounds sterling, out of which are paid the salaries of the Speaker of the House of Representatives and of the secretaries; the remainder is destined to meet the expence which local circumstances may require for the service and maintnance of society.

W. R. Riddell, ed., *op. cit.*, p. 39.

14) Everything is excessively dear at Newark. The shops are few, and the shopkeepers, combining against the public, fix what price they choose upon their goods. The high duty laid by England upon all the commodities exported from her islands proves a powerful encouragement to a contraband trade with the United States, where, in many articles, the difference of price amounts to two-thirds. The government of Canada is very vigilant to prevent this contraband trade; but a certain prospect of gain excites to exertion, which will frequently succeed in eluding the law, as well as the vigilance of the executive power. The shopkeepers know perfectly well how to favour this contraband trade, the only means for destroying which would be to lower the duties, and, of consequence, the price of the commodities. The Governor has it in contemplation, to encourage such manufactures as produce these articles, which are *run* in large quantities into this province from the United States, such as hats. But all his exertions to this effect will fail in regard to sugar, coffee, tea; in short, with respect to all commodities, which are directly imported from the United States, without being there subjected to as high a duty as in Canada.

Ibid., pp. 43-44.

[1] Four dollars.

3.   Pioneer Social Institutions

If you know the name of the Lieutenant-Governor of your province you are one of a small percentage of the people in your province who do. Today the office of Lieutenant-Governor is a constitutional necessity but of little real consequence in the decision-making processes of government. Perhaps the most famous, and certainly among the most dynamic and talented Lieutenant-Governors of Ontario, was the first, John Graves Simcoe.

A soldier of renown, Simcoe rose to the command of his own unit, the Queen's Rangers, during the Revolutionary war, and in July of 1792 took the oath of office as Lieutenant-Governor of Upper Canada. Always a controversial figure, he remains to this day an historical personality of dispute. To some he was a great man, to others a self seeking opportunist. But most will agree, that his impact upon the formative years of Upper Canada, for good or ill, was great.

La Rochefoucault described Simcoe in this way:

> But for his inveterate hatred against the United States, which he too loudly professes, and which carries him too far, General Simcoe appears in the most advantageous light. He is just, active, enlightened, brave, frank, and possesses the confidence of the country, of the troops, and of all those who join him in the administration of public affairs. To these he attends with the closest application; he preserves all the old friends of the King, and neglects no means to procure him new ones. He unites, in my judgment, all the qualities which his station requires, to maintain the important possession of Canada, if it be possible that England can long retain it.[1]

This section will help you to determine to what extent the social order of Upper Canada conformed to his plans.

---

1. Give an account of the values held by Simcoe, taking into consideration his role in the Revolutionary war, as well as events in Britain and France in the 1780's and 1790's.

2. How does this avowed "Yankee-hater" justify his invitation to Americans to help populate Upper Canada?

3. How does Simcoe propose to defend the colony while at the same time promote social stability?

[1] Riddell, *op. cit.*, p. 38.

4. By examining Simcoe's views and those of Cartwright, suggest what they consider to be the qualities of an ideal settler.

5. In what way is the American question, faced by Simcoe, similar to problems faced by our federal and provincial governments today?

1) Simcoe's Grand Design
Simcoe to Dundas, June 30, 1791

It appears to me that the Colony of Upper Canada in its original form should contain within itself an Epitome of those Establishments, Civil & Military, which must be gradually but necessarily extended hereafter as it shall encrease in numbers, in political & commercial consequence & become capable of supporting its own expences or contributing to those of the Empire & that the utmost Attention should be paid that British Customs, Manners, & Principles in the most trivial as well as serious matters should be promoted & inculcated to obtain their due Ascendancy to assimilate the Colony with the parent state & to bear insensibly all their habitual Influence in the Support of that British Constitution which has been so wisely extended to that Country. . . .

I hold it to *be determined* upon & incontrovertible that Great Britain is to maintain her Possession of Canada.

Cruickshank, *The Simcoe Papers*, I, p. 27.

2) Simcoe on Immigration

There are thousands of the Inhabitants of the United States whose affections are centered in the British Government & the British Name; who are positively enemies of Congress[1] & to the late division of the Empire, many of their Connections have already taken refuge in Canada & it will be true Wisdom to invite & facilitate the emigration of this description of people into that Country.

It being obvious that from such Emigrants, their Descendants (& in some measure all classes of People) will adopt that habitual attachment to the British Nation which is a great bond of Union between the Subjects of any State & a powerful Barrier against any attempts which may be made to overthrow or undermine the existing form of Government, nor let it be supposed that this aversion from Congress, . . . , if rightly improved on, has or is near dying away; the contest of the natives of Great Britain with the Subjects of the American States was decided by Arms & terminated by Treaty.

That of the American with the American still exists under all the injurious Remembrances of open or covert Vexation under the Taunts of triumph, taxes, & family Confiscations.

Other classes of Americans will emigrate to better their fortunes & whose Indifference to any form of Government may be converted into zealous attach-

[1] The American government's legislative branch. The House of Representatives was elected on the basis of representation by population and the Senate, until 1913, was composed of two Senators per state and elected by the states.

ment to that under which they shall live, whenever they shall feel the advantages of its beneficence & Wisdom, of the Equality of its Laws & its protection from the *probability* of *foreign Invasion*. Emigration of hardy, industrious & virtuous Men may be reasonably expected from the northern parts of Great Britain.

> *Ibid.*, I, p. 27.

3) Simcoe's Class Structure
Simcoe to Sir Joseph Banks

I mean to prepare for whatever Convulsions may happen in the United States, and the Method I propose is by establishing a free, honourable British Government, and a pure Administration of its Laws, which shall hold out to the solitary Emigrant, and to the several States, advantages that the present form of Government doth not and cannot permit them to enjoy. There are inherent Defects in the Congressional form of Government, the absolute prohibition of an order of Nobility is a glaring one. The true New England Americans have as strong an Aristocratical spirit as is to be found in Great Britain; nor are they Anti-monarchial. I hope to have a hereditary Council with some mark of Nobility.

> *Ibid.*, I, p. 17.

4) Simcoe's Religious Establishment
Simcoe to Dundas, June 30, 1791

I hold it to be indispensably necessary that a Bishop should be immediately established in Upper Canada.

The State Propriety of some form of Public Worship, politically considered, arises from the necessity there is of preventing enthusiastick & fanatick Teachers from acquiring that superstitious hold of the minds of the multitude which Persons of such a description may pervert. . . . Those who shall be bred in solitude & seclusion which the first settlers must necessarily be, & to whom perhaps the stated periods of publick Worship are the only ones in which in their meetings & associations they shall become acquainted & sympathize with each other. Such a Description of men will be the fittest Instruments for the mischief making Enthusiasm of the Sectaries[1] to work upon and this at a Period when we know that all Men read & only one description of People write; & when the Aim of the Sectaries is avowedly to destroy the national establishment[2].

At this very moment we see Episcopacy happily introduced or introducing into all the United States, nor in Parliament or the Canada Bill have we seen any objections taken to the Episcopal Function, which was supposed to take place of course, but to the admission of the Bishop to a seat of the Legislature, which it is to be hoped, while there is an Establishment, the Wisdom of this Country will always insist upon.

[1] Sectaries were supporters of non-Anglican Protestant churches, such as Methodists.
[2] The Church of England.

There are duties of Office in respect to the Laity of the Church of England which a Bishop only can perform. It is of the most serious importance that his power & supervision over the Clergy should prevent or censure clerical offences & inculcate thro' all Ranks & Descriptions of People a sober, an industrious & religious & conscientious spirit, which will be the best security that Government can have for its own internal preservation. Schools & Seminaries of Education must be created or there will be no considerable Emigration. These should be under the Superintendency of the Bishop, without this Head The Levelling Spirit would infect the very teachers of the Episcopal Church. . . .

Ibid., I, pp. 31-32.

5) Simcoe on Education
Simcoe to Dundas, April 28, 1792

– But, Sir, there is an Object of very great and momentous Policy to which I hope you will give due consideration, . . . ; I mean an immediate and due provision for the education of the superior classes of the Country, such education as may be necessary for people in the lower degrees of life, necessarily requiring but little expence, may be at present provided for by their Connections and relations, . . . but schools of education necessary for the higher classes, being of greater expence and requiring instantaneous establishment, must depend upon the liberality of the British government; Upper Canada having no revenue at present from whence these necessary purposes can be supplied, necessity will compel and the cheapness of education in the United States without some internal establishment will invite the Gentlemen of Upper Canada to send their children thither for education by which means from habit from intercourse, and assiduous design in their Instructors, their British Principles will be perverted, . . . and subverted by different principles being instilled into the rising generation, . . .

Ibid., I, p. 143.

6) Simcoe's Social Cement

Yet, by his account, the prevailing sentiments of the people render the admission of new inhabitants, who present themselves, rather difficult; especially of those, who come from the United States. For this reason, he[1] sends such colonists, as cannot give a satisfactory account of themselves, into the back country, and stations soldiers on the banks of the lakes, which are in front of them. He would admit every superannuated[2] soldier of the English army, and all officers of long service, who are on half-pay, to share in the distribution of such lands as the King had a right to dispose of. He would dismiss every soldier, now quartered in Canada, and give him one hundred acres of land, as soon as he should procure a young man to serve as his substitute. With his views to encrease the population of the country, he blends the design of drawing young

[1] Simcoe
[2] retired

Americans into the English service, by which he will augment the number of American families, attached to the King of Great Britain. In the midst of these families of soldiers, which he intends to settle on the lakes, and on all the frontiers towards the United States, he means to place all the officers, who as has already been observed, have any claim on the lands. He proposes thus to form a militia, attached to the King from habit and gratitude; and this he considers as one of the most certain means for suppressing the disturbances, which might be excited by some disaffected new settlers, who inhabit the mid-land counties, and at the same time as one of the best measures of defence in case of an attack. By this plan of settling amidst the soldiers officers and gentlemen of respectable families, whom he hopes to attract from England, he wishes to form a class of gentry,[1] and to promote more or less the execution of the project, clearly discernible in the new constitution, to introduce into the two Canadas an hereditary nobility.

Riddell ed., *op. cit.*, pp. 30-31.

4.   Immigration

1. Why is the term "Late Loyalist" inappropriate to describe Americans who settled in Upper Canada after 1791?

2. Why would Americans find less difficulty in adjusting to Upper Canada than immigrants from the British Isles?

3. Compare Cartwright's views, with those of Simcoe and indicate where their views agree and disagree.

1) The "Late Loyalists" by Richard Cartwright in 1795

It must be admitted that the Americans understood the mode of agriculture proper for a new country better than any other people, and being, from necessity, in the habit of providing with their own hands many things which in other countries the artizan is always at hand to supply, they possess resources in themselves which other people are usually strangers to; and boldly began their operations in a wilderness, when the dreary novelty of the situation would appal an European. But their political notions in general are as exceptionable as their intelligence and hardihood are deserving of praise. I am not, however, inclined to impute to such of them as emigrate to this Province either hostile or treacherous views; but it would be an error equally as great to suppose that they are induced by any preference they entertain for our government. They come probably with no other intent than to better their circumstances, by acquiring lands upon easy terms. Now, it is not to be expected that a man

[1] people of rank in society

will change his political principles or prejudices by crossing a river, or that an oath of allegiance is at once to check his bias of the mind, and prevent the predilection for those maxims and modes of estimating and conducting the concerns of the public to which he has been trained, from displaying itself, even without any sinister purpose, whenever an opportunity shall be presented.

C. E. Cartwright, *op. cit.*, p. 96.

1. What are the values of these settlers?
2. Why did the Highland Scots prove to be successful settlers?
3. Why did they not progress as rapidly as settlers from the United States?
4. Why would circumstances in Europe between 1793 and 1815 prevent any large scale European emigration?

2) The Highland Scots[1] – Lord Selkirk's[2] Diary, January 22, 1804

Mr. Bethune[3] speaks of the Settlers in Glengarry as labourious & economical – sending to market many articles which the English Settlers consume – They use less flesh meat, & less bread, more Potatoes, garden vegetables, milk etc. – The old Settlers do not equal the Americans, but the young men who have come over children are as expert as any at the axe – They all he thinks are more assiduous at work than the Amns.[4] & allow themselves less indulgence – yet from the want of habit they have not got thro' the work that might have been done – perhaps in part from their living all together which has given them less opportunity of learning soon the modes of carrying on work, adapted to the country. – The old Settlers are in general comfortably lodged tho' not in the style that Amns. of the same standing would – no framed houses but good squared log, well fitted & tight – good doors & windows, chimneys & stoves – the house about 30 or more feet in front with a garret or half second story – generally with upright windows – their accomodation fully as good as the farmers of 100 or 150 a year in Galloway – These squared log houses are mortised at the corners – the walls, shingling etc. are done by the people themselves with the assistance of rough country carpentery (from among themselves) for flooring – windows doors etc. The original log house of a much poorer appearance, is generally remaining at a short distance – the later settlers . . . have not got beyond the first log house. – These accommodations appear poor to the Amern. & English Settlers but they are a wonderful advance from the Hovels of Glengarry, & the advance in cleanliness seems to keep pace with

[1] In 1786 five hundred Highlanders arrived at Glengarry in Prescott County.
[2] Son of a Scottish nobleman who gained fame as a colonizer in Prince Edward Island, Upper Canada and the Red River settlement in the northwest territories.
[3] John Bethune (1751-1815) a Minister of the Church of Scotland, was clergyman to the Glengarry settlers after 1787.
[4] Americans.

that of houses. The Settlers have all their Slays[1] for going to Church etc. as well as for work – they are very cheap & easily built – They make a good deal of Cloth – all their own wear, except a little fine cloth which is bought for Sunday dress – there is no fulling[2] mill nearer than Long Saut, but the women full with their feet in the old fashion described by Tennant – Sr. J. Johnston has a valuable grist & saw mill just bye Mr. B's meeting house – there are one or two others in the Settlement. . . .

> P. C. T. White, *Lord Selkirk's Diary: 1803-1804*, P.A.C. MS. 19, Vol. 79, Diary No. 3, pp. 716-722.

1. What was Talbot's relationship to Simcoe? How might this relationship have influenced Talbot's motives for promoting colonization?

2. Why did the British government encourage Talbot's venture?

3. On what terms was he to receive his land grant? Why did the government insist upon his giving fifty acres to each family "he may claim"?

3) Talbot Settlement
Colonial Office to Lieutenant Governor Hunter,[3]
15th February, 1803

Sir,

Several proposals have lately been submitted to the consideration of His Majesty's government, from persons who with different objects in view are desirous of employing their resources and exertions in the settlement and cultivation of lands in Canada.

Among the individuals who have addressed themselves to me upon this subject, Mr. Talbot[4] who acted as private Secretary to Lieutenant General Simcoe in Upper Canada, appears not only from his character and military services, but from the accurate knowledge of the Province which during a long residence there, he has personally acquired, as well as from the nature of his plans, to merit particular attention.

This gentleman having already made some successful attempts in the cuture of hemp,[5] purposes to direct his attention to the growth and preparation of that valuable plant, and by his influence and example to promote and extend its cultivation, particularly among those settlers he conceives he may be able to introduce into the Colony, and to establish in his neighborhood.

He has therefore applied for a grant of land in the distant township of Yarmouth, in the County of Norfolk, on Lake Erie, as being from the nature of the soil, favorable to his design of raising hemp for exportation, and also

[1] sleighs
[2] The process of cleansing and thickening cloth by beating or washing.
[3] The Lieutenant-Governor in 1799 who remained in office until 1805 without making any significant imprint on the colony.
[4] Thomas Talbot.
[5] The fibres of hemp are used for sailcloth and rope.

affording scope for the establishment of such a number of families as may be induced to follow him into the Province.

In consequence of the assurances which have been received that Mr. Talbot is in every respect qualified to prosecute the undertaking; I am commanded by His Majesty to authorise you to take the proper steps for passing without delay, according to the usual form, and subject to the customary reservations, a grant of five thousand acres in his favor in the township above mentioned, . . . You are at the same time to give directions that a proportion of such township immediately contiguous to Mr. Talbot's grant, may for the present be reserved for the purpose of hereafter appropriating to him according to circumstances, a further quantity at the rate of two hundred acres for every family he may induce to settle there, either from the continent of Europe, or America; – provided he shall have surrendered fifty acres of his original grant to each family for which he may claim, and that such family shall at the time, be established in the actual possession of the said fifty acres.

I enclose a copy of Lieut. General Simcoe's letter to me, forwarding Mr. Talbot's application, and from the high terms in which he is therein mentioned, I am induced to recommend him to your protection and good offices – . . .

I must request you will favor me with your opinion how far it may be advisable with a view to the speedy settlement of the waste lands in the Province under your government, to make further grants upon the principle described in this letter. . . .

> As quoted in *Select Documents in Canadian Economic History 1783-1885*, edited by H. A. Innes and A. R. M. Lower (Toronto: The University of Toronto Press, 1933), pp. 23-24.

5.   Patterns of Settlement before 1812

1. Using an outline map of present day Ontario and the following description, indicate the extent of settlement by 1812.

2. From the descriptions of Upper Canada villages as they existed in 1812, suggest reasons for their being chosen as population centres.

3. Judging by the activities and buildings of these villages, what are the differences which might exist between the attitudues and values of the village and those of rural inhabitants?

1) Settlements

In the lower part of this province, the settlements do not extend back or north from the river St. Lawrence. Above Kingston, the settlements extend from Lake Ontario, 50 miles. Above the head of the bay,[1] on the lake shore, for

---

[1] Quinté

about 100 miles, the settlements do not extend more than 6 miles from the lake. North from York, the settlements extend farther back, particularly on what is called Yonge-Street, which runs a due north course to Lake Simcoe. On both sides of this street, the farms are thick and well improved, the soil being very good, although the climate is not so favourable as it is farther to the southwest. From York, west, along the lake shore, there are but small settlements on the shore for 20 miles; after which, what is called Dundas-Street, 4 miles from the shore, is thickly settled on both sides for twenty miles; as also between this and the lake it is thinly inhabited, although this has not been settled more than 6 years from the present date (1812). Above 10 or 15 miles, at the head of Burlington bay, is what is called Goot's[1] Paradise. It is fine, rich, sandy plains, thickly settled 7 miles from the shore, to the foot of the slope already named; and on the top, west and north-west for 15 miles, there are fine settlements in two townships – East and West Flambeau.[2] Farther south around the head of Lake Ontario, or more particularly Burlington bay, the settlements are thick, extending west 16 miles. About 40 miles up the Grand River is a thick settlement of Dutch, in Brant's township. Still to the east, as the road leads to Niagara, the settlements are thick near the shore of Lake Ontario.

After one gets 30 miles east of the head of Burlington bay, and 20 from Niagara, the settlements of an old date are made, and pretty thick, all the way across from lake to lake, which is more than thirty miles. From the thick settlement west of the head of lake Ontario, towards the London district, the inhabitants are thin for 20 miles, through the tract of land belonging to the six nations of Indians . . .

Villages

There are not many villages, in the province of Upper Canada of much note, the inhabitants finding their greatest advantage in agriculture, as the land is very cheap and fertile. . . .

Niagara

It is a beautiful and prospective place, being surrounded on two sides by water, the lake on the north, and the Niagara river on the east, and which affords a fine harbour for shipping.

Fort George of this place stands about half a mile from the mouth of this river, . . . ; it is nearly square, enclosing a space of about 150 yards long and an 100 broad. The pickets are high and strong, defended by a ditch on the out side, and breast works on the inside. It is well provided with cannon, ammunition, water, provision and the like. This village is a place of much trade, and is inhabited by a civil and industrious people. It contains a council-house, court-house, and jail, and 2 houses for public worship. There are several squares of ground in this village adorned with almost every kind of precious fruit. The front part of the village, on the east, looks towards the fort over a beautiful plain of nearly 1 mile wide.

[1] Coote's
[2] Flamboro

Kingston

Stands a few miles below the head of the St. Lawrence, opposite to an Island
which is the means of forming a safe and commodious harbour. It contains
about 150 houses, a court-house, jail, and 2 houses for public worship. The
fort in this place is temporary, the cannon are small. It is a place of much trade.
There are several more small villages on the banks of the bay of Quantie,[1]
and are places of some trade, all of which increase and flourish rapidly.

York[2]

Is situated 170 miles south west of Kingston, on the north shore of Lake
Ontario, and is something larger than the former. This village is laid out after
the form of Philadelphia, the streets crossing each other at right angles; though
the ground on which it stands is not suitable for building. This at present is
the seat of government, and the residence of a number of English gentlemen.
It contains some fine buildings, though they stand scattering, among which
are a court-house, council-house, a large brick building in which the king's
store for the place is kept, and a meeting-house for Episcopalians,[3] 1 printing,
and other offices. This city lies in north latitude 43 degrees and some minutes.
The harbour in front of the city is commodious, safe and beautiful, and is
formed after a curious manner . . . About 300 yards from the shore, and as
many from the fort, there is a channel through this circular island merely
sufficient for the passage of large vessels. This bason, which in the middle is
2 miles wide, is very deep and without rocks, or any thing of the kind . . . The
fort in this place is not strong, but the British began to build a very strong one
in the year 1811.

> M. Smith, *A Geographical View of the Province of Upper Canada*
> (Philadelphia, October 1813), provided courtesy of Burlington Local
> History Project.

1. After examining the following sources, write a short essay entitled
   "Life at York before 1812."

2. Why did Simcoe choose York as the site for his capital?

2) Life in an Upper Canadian Town
Lord Selkirk's Opinion of York

Sunday 20th. [November, 1803] . . . York contains 60 or 70 houses – the first
built part is compact the lots being 1/5 acre each – latterly acre lots have been
granted & several to one person – also evasions of the condition of building on
each have been allowed so that the new or Western part of the Town is very
scattered – the roads called streets infamous & almost impassable – the whole
appears very ragged from the Stumps – near the Eastern end of the Town is
a blockhouse built by President Russel on an alarm from Brant's Indians – &

[1] Quinté
[2] Toronto
[3] Anglicans

near it the situation proposed for a Governor's House – where only two rooms are built that serve from the meeting of Assembly, Courts of Justice etc. This situation is found to be unhealthy from the neighbourhood of a marsh of 1000 acres formed by the mouth of the Don – this marsh is not found to affect the Garrison or more distant part of the Town at about a mile or mile & half distant – A party of Soldiers stationed in the Block house last summer were constantly affected by Fever and Ague,[1] while the Garrison on a dry bank 2 miles off was quite healthy – the old town was also more unhealthy than the new part which is farther from the Marsh – & up in Yonge Street a few miles from the Town no fever at all existed. – The prevalence of Easterly winds last summer blowing off the marsh rendered the Town more than usually unhealthy – . . . The Seat of Govt. was removed to York in a slap dash manner soon after the Posts were given up – Niagara has been chosen by Genl. Simcoe under the idea of the land to the Genesee & being retained by Britain[2] & when disappointed of this, he would not hold his Parliament under the Guns of an American Fortress – he had an aversion at Kingston, partly because Lord Dorchr[3] approved of it, but principally because all the lands were taken up around it – York had the advantage of being able to afford lots for all his friends round it, & accordingly the lands for some miles distance are all in the hands of Officers of Govt. etc. etc. – & generally remain unimproved. – The Officers of Govt. were obliged to remove from comfortable houses at Niagara into an absolute wood where people were sometimes losing themselves between one hut & another – some incamped till near Christmas, before they could get Loghouses from the want of hands & the run upon the few workmen that could be got – wages & building materials continued for two or three years at double rates – Genl. S.[4] was careless of personal accommodation himself. . . .

Most of the lands between York & Bay of Quinté are taken up in large lots, & there are so few Settlers that the country is nearly impassable, as it also it thro' the Mississaga lands to the Westward towards the head of the Lake – So that York remains an insulated spot almost detached from both ends of the province, – the roads are so bad that in Summer everybody prefers a passage across the Lake – a strange situation for a Capital! . . .

There is no regular Post to Upper Canada from Quebec except 4 Couriers once a month in Winter – in summer letters are trusted to occasional opportunities. . . . A workman's board at York without liquor may be had for 1½ $ per week for 2 or 3 years after the beginning of the Town not under 3½ or 4$ – flour was then 16$ per barrel. –

To get an idea of the expense of building, I put a sketch of a house on a common place plan – 30 by 40 – 2 stories (20 feet sidewall) cellar & garret[5] – into two Carpenters hands to give Estimates. –

[1] An acute fever.
[2] Simcoe hoped that Britain would retain a number of forts including Niagara in American territory. These posts were given up to the Americans in 1796 as part of Jay's Treaty.
[3] Lord Dorchester.
[4] Simcoe
[5] an attic

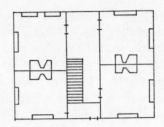

J. Leach estimates – £920 N.Y.C.[1] . . .

Templeton estimates a similar house . . . N.Y.C.   £1065 . 2 . 5

. . . . .

The builders here have an idea that a log house cannot be built to last well, as all Log houses they have seen are apt to settle & get out of shape – owing no doubt to the use of unseasoned wood, & to the want of underpinning or a stone foundation. Some few houses are filled up with brick between the frame, but the generality not – & they have a number of cold windows – the seasons are not severe enough to make them attend to comfort. –

There are some beautiful species of Timber made use of in furniture & ornamental house furnishing – Black Walnut, Curled Maple, & Cherry – these are sometimes sent down St. Lawrence for exportation. . . .

P. C. T. White, *op. cit.*, pp. 19623-19668.

3) Theatrical Performance in York

Exhibition

Messrs. Potter & Thompson,

from London,

Take the Liberty of informing the Ladies and Gentlemen of York and its vicinity, that they will perform at Mr. Miller's Assembly-Room, formerly the Toronto Coffee-House, on Monday the 7th instant,

Philosophical, Mathematical and Curious Experiments,

many of which were never performed in America by any others but themselves; Theatrical performance, consisting of Songs and Recitations and

Ventriloquism.

In the course of the evening will be sung the following Songs, the Straw Bonnet, the much admired Song of the Cosmetic Doctor, or the man for the Ladies, Caleb Quotern or the man of all Trades and Giles Crogans Ghost, by Mr. Potter, with an accompaniment on the Violin by Mr. Lyon.

Tickets to be had at the place of performance. Front seats half a Dollar., back seats half price. for further particulars see Bills.

York, 4th May, 1810.

York Gazette, May 5, 1810.

[1] New York currency

4) Joseph Willcocks[1] to Richard Willcocks,[2] Dublin

Upper Cana York
3d. November 1800

There are several Irishmen here and to the Honor of our Country the first and
only Man that has been hung here was an Irishman, it happened since I came
here it was for Forgery, there was no getting a Hangman untill at length an other
dear Countryman who was in for Robbery, with the promise of a Pardon and
twenty Guineas to carry him out of the Country filled the Office with the most
unpardonable Ignorance, the Gentleman who was to die fell three times from
the Gallows – it fulfilled the old adage – put an Irishman on the spit and you
will get another to turn him. . . . Labourers Wages here are extravagantly high,
never less than from 6 to 10 Irish Shillings a day, Carpenters & Masons from
9 to 14 these Wages are general thro' America, sometimes more but never less,
so that no Man can make Money except those who have large families that
can Labor. In this Province Mutten is 6½d and Beef 4d the poind In Lower
Canad Mutten 2½ Beef 1½d a Boushell of Potatoes 2d. bread 1d a lb but
Groceries very high and Waring Apparel excessively high I paid 5s a yard for a
piece of Irish Linen Yesterday, at home it would be three, Madaira 2s2d per
quart & Cheaper, Claret is not drank here, Port good 1s.10d a quart – The
heat of Summer is insupportable & the Cold of Winter Intollerable, there are
many instances of Persons being frozen to death and a Winter does not pass
by with out several noses, fingers, and feet being lost, for my part I dred the
Winter altho I have one of the most Comfortable rooms in this Province there
is no such room in Donougmores House, in fact Mr. Russell[3] thinks nothing
to good for me. We have an elegant pair of Horses, and a Sled that will be
find Sport in Winter if not too Cold, but we have a great many very valuable
Skins some of which are for the purpose of Sleding. . . .

P.A.O., Willcock's Letter Book, Part One, pp. 28-32.

5) Russell[3] to Sheriff Alexander McDonell,

York 12 May 1798

However your Letter of this date and the Conversation I have had with you
upon the subject convincing me that it will be very soon impossible to restrain
the Enormities of this increasing Town so as to secure the Peace and safety
of its Inhabitants unless some other Provision is made which may be executed
in less time than a District Jail is likely to require; I judge it to be my Duty

[1] Joseph Willcocks arrived at York in 1800, where he rose to the
position of sheriff of the Home district, only to be dismissed for his
association with Judge Thorpe in 1807. He subsequently edited an
anti-government newspaper and deserted to the United States in
1812. He was killed fighting for the Americans.
[2] Richard was Joseph Willcock's brother.
[3] Peter Russell served as Administrator in Upper Canada between
the administrations of Simcoe, who departed for England in 1796,
and Hunter's arrival in August 1799.

during the present recess of the Council to authorise you (after consulting with Capt. Graham) to cause a small log building to be erected of sufficient strength and size to secure three separate Prisoners, and accomodate the Keeper. – you will likewise be pleased to provide Handcuffs and other Irons for binding gross Offenders, and stocks for punishing those who may deserve such Chastisement. – The Expence attending this Service will be discharged on your Requisition by my Warrant on the Receiver General of the Province –

Toronto Public Library, Peter Russell Papers.

6.   Religion in Upper Canada before 1812

1. From the following sources, identify the religious groups which established themselves in Upper Canada.

2. What rivalries existed between religious groups? Why?

3. What evidence do these sources provide to explain the success of the Methodist church in Upper Canada? How did the circuit riders contribute to this success?

4. What was the relationship of the Church of England to the government? Why were Methodists particularly condemned by the government? What is an established church?

5. How might Simcoe have reacted to the condition of religion in Upper Canada in 1812?

1) The Origins of the "Established" Church
Stuart [1] to Mathews:[2] Montreal, 14th July, 1784

Having ever since my arrival in this Province Experienced his Excellency the Commander in Chief's Patronage & peculiar Indulgence, I consider myself accountable to him for my Conduct & the Disposition of my Time; – impressed with this Idea, I think it my Duty to acquaint his Excellency that, agreeable to my Intention mentioned in a former Letter I have visited Niagara, the Mohawk Village Butler's-bury, the Bay of Quintie, Cataraqui, and every Encampment of Loyalists down to Coteau Du Lac, and baptized the children presented in each Place, the whole Number amounting to near 150.

I arrived at Cataraqui Time enough to see the Lots drawn, and Mr Grass's Corps indulged me with the Choice of a lot within a mile of the Barracks with which I am well satisfied. – I have ordered some Improvement to be made immediately & mean to remove my Family thither early next Spring. – I beg Leave to observe that I have lately received a Letter from the Society notifying

[1] See footnote on page 6.
[2] Governor Haldimand's secretary.

to me that my Salary of £70 pr Ann: for the Mohawks is reduced to £50; and the Society are pleased to place so much Confidence in me as to leave the Place of my future Residence in Canada, to my own Choice. I intend to inform then that I am determined to fix at Cataraqui; But as I have nothing more than £50 to expect from the Society, I hope his Excellency will not consider it as a matter of idle Curiosity, if I wish to know whether he has had a proper opportunity of recommending me for the Chaplaincy. For that once ascertained I shall rest perfectly contented, being as certain of Success, as if I were already possessed of the appointment. However if you think my Request improper I must beg the Favor of you not to communicate the contents of this Letter, and you will confer an additional Obligation on him who is already [etc.] . . .

P.A.C., Haldimand MSS., B162, pp. 333-4.

2) The Bishop of Quebec to Henry Dundas[1]
Powell Place, Quebec, 15 Sept. 1794
Report of a Journey to Upper Canada

With respect to Religious Instruction the state of these settlers is, for the most part, truly deplorable. From Montreal to Kingston, a distance of 200 miles, there is not one Clergyman of the Church of England, nor any house of Religious Worship except one small Ch belonging to the Lutherans & one or perhaps two belonging to the Presbyterians. The Public Worship of God is entirely suspended or performed in a manner which can neither tend to improve the people in Religious Truth nor to render them useful members of Society. The Presbyterian[2] & the L[utheran] Clergm[3] are, I believe, men of good character, but their influence is necessarily limited to their own little congregations. The greatest bulk of the people have and can have no instruction but such as they receive occasionally from itinerant and mendicant Methodists, a set of ignorant enthusiasts, whose preaching is calculated only to perplex the understanding, & corrupt the morals & relax the nerves of industry, & disolve the bonds of society.

At Kingston there is a small but decent church, a respectable congregation (much too numerous to be properly seated in it) & a Minister greatly, & justly esteem'd by the people. . . .

P.A.C. Mountain Papers, Q69-2, p. 385.

3) The First Methodist Preacher: 1790?
A Traditional Story of the Arrival of William Losee[4]

It was to labor and suffer in this remote region and among the settlers in such circumstances that the first missionaries of the Methodist Episcopal

[1] Henry Dundas was Secretary of State for Home Affairs.
[2] John Bethune.
[3] Samuel Schwedfeger preached in the county of Dundas from 1790 till his death in 1803.
[4] First Methodist preacher in Upper Canada. He travelled between New York State and Upper Canada from 1790 to 1816.

Church penetrated the woods and swamps intervening between the settlements in the States and Canada.

I recollect conversing nearly forty years since, with an old sister Van Camp who was among first fruits of Methodism in Canada. She told me that she had her residence at first in the township of Cornwall and in the winter of 1791, or thereabouts she saw through her window one exceedingly severe day a snowstorm then raging a man on horseback who knocked at her door and asked shelter and the rites of hospitality. Being a stranger almost famished, she took him in and accomodated him as well as able. He then told her he was a Methodist Missionary named Loscend[1] after he had been refreshed he would preach that very night if the people could be collected. She seconded the motion cheerfully, though quite a stranger to the Methodists and sent her boys out to notify the neighbors. Thus was preaching and worship introduced into those parts and she soon became a happy convert to the faith taught and so strikingly exemplified in the labors, sufferings, boldness and zeal of the herald of it.

> *Reminiscence of the Reverend James Richardson, D.D.*
> (Douglas Library, Queen's University), p. 36.

4) Stuart to the Bishop of Nova Scotia
Kingston, March 5, 1790

Two itinerant Preachers, of the Methodist Class, are now in this Settlement. – the one is called McCarty[2], the Person I mentioned to you; – he is an illiterate Irishman; and a Man of an infamous private Character. – I think, we will be able to banish him for Crimes of a henious Nature. – the other is just arrived, – his name is Loosey, – he says he has been in Nova Scotia & pretends to be acquainted with you. – He has the same Recommendation as the other; that is, he has formerly been a Man of a very bad moral Character. But his Conversion is therefore the greater Miracle and he will be the better able to preach *experimental* Doctrine. – I have taken no steps to oppose either of them; being well convinced that their Reign will be short, if they cannot provoke Persecution. . . .

> Anglican Synod of Ontario, *Stuart Letters.*

5) A Methodist Revival

In Upper Canada a gracious revival commenced in 1797 chiefly through the the instrumentality of Hezekiah Calvin Wooster.[3] At a quarterly meeting on the Bay of Quinte Circuit, after preaching on Saturday, while the presiding elder, Darius Dunham,[4] retired with the official brethren to hold the quarterly conference, Mr. Wooster remained in the meeting to pray with some who were under awakenings, and others who were groaning for full redemption in

---

[1] Losee.
[2] A Methodist convert from Catholicism who came to Upper Canada in 1788.
[3] A Methodist preacher in the Bay of Quinté circuits from 1796-1798.
[4] A Methodist preacher who came to Upper Canada in 1792 and left the ministry in 1800.

the blood of the Lamb. While uniting with his brethren in this exercise, the power of the Most High seemed to overshadow the congregation, and many were filled with joy unspeakable, and were praising the Lord for what he had done for their souls, while others, with "speechless awe and silent love," were prostrate on the floor. When the presiding elder came into the house, he beheld these things with a mixture of wonder and indignation, believing that "wild-fire" was burning among the people. After gazing awhile with silent astonishment, he kneeled down, and began to pray God to stop the "raging of the wild-fire" as he called it. In the meantime, Calvin Wooster, whose soul was burning with the "fire of the Holy Ghost", kneeled by the side of Dunham, and while the latter was earnestly engaged in prayer for God to put out the wild-fire, Wooster softly whispered out a prayer in the following words: "Lord, bless Brother Dunham! Lord, bless Brother Dunham!" Thus they continued for some minutes, when at length the prayer of Brother Wooster prevailed, and Dunham fell prostrate on the floor; and ere he rose, received a baptism of that very fire, which he had feelingly deprecated as the effect of a wild imagination. There was now harmony in their prayers . . .

Bang's *History of the Methodist Episcopal Church*, quoted in J. B. Wakely, *The Heroes of Methodism* (New York: 1856).

6) Bishop Mountain on the State of the Established Church

Compared with the respectable Establishments, the substantial revenues, and the extensive powers and privileges, of the Church of Rome, the Church of England sinks into a merely tolerated sect; possessing at the present moment, not one shilling of revenue which it can properly call its own; without laws to control the conduct of its members, or even to regulate the ordinary proceedings of Vestries[1] and Church-Wardens; without any provision for organizing or conducting the necessary proceedings of an Ecclesiastical Court, or power to enforce their execution. And what is worst of all, and what cannot but alarm and afflict the mind of every serious and reflecting man, without a body of clergy, either by their number sufficient for the exigencies of the State, or by any acknowledged right, or legitimate authority, capable of maintaining their own usefulness or supporting the dignity of a Church Establishment.

. . . In both Provinces the majority of His Majesty's Protestant subjects are Dissenters; and of these there is a great variety of Sects: I speak not only my own opinion (sir), but that of many of the best informed persons in both Provinces when I say that an effectual and respectable *Establishment* of the Church of England would go near to unite the whole body of Dissenters, within its pale.

P.A.C., *Q Series*, XCII: Quebec, June 6, 1803, Bishop Mountain to Lieutenant-Governor Milnes.

7) Progress and Influence of Methodism

[In 1791] one Episcopal Clergyman at Kingston, another in Bath, and a third in Niagara, constituted the sole religious instructors of the country. As

[1] A group who manage church business affairs.

for Methodism, it was only known by hear-say to the dispersed inhabitants, as a subject of ridicule and scorn. Its principles were deemed absurd; its services and society meetings were ridiculed as enthusiastic; its Ministers were viewed as ignorant, idle, hypocritical adventurers, and political spies; some of them fell victims to Magisterial persecution; up to a very recent period, Methodism has been regarded by many leading Magistrates and other civil officers through-out the Province, and by most prominent members of the Executive Government, as dangerous to the supremacy of British power; and the combined influence of men of wealth and learning, together with the Civil Government itself, from the Representative of the King (with few exceptions) down to the Church Sexton, has been arrayed against the progress of Methodism, and bent, as far as the spirit of the age would permit, upon its extermination.

Such were the circumstances under which the standard of Methodism was raised in this Province; and such are the formidable obstacles which have opposed its progress. It had no pecuniary resources but the voluntary liberality of those who embraced its principles. Its doctrines and precepts waged war with the prevalent vices and popular prejudices of the country. Its teachers were men of humble rank, as well as of humble literary or educational pre-tensions. . . . In the spirit of primitive Christianity those devoted men went forth, not counting their lives dear unto them, but in weariness and poverty, in the extremes of heat and cold, at all seasons and in all kinds of weather – sometimes whole nights in the wilderness, surrounded by the wild beasts of the desert, – they traced their way by blazed trees and Indian bye-paths, and forded creeks and rivers – in some instances at the risk of their lives – to testify to the pioneer settlers of the country "the glorious Gospel of God our Saviour," . . .

Viewing the progress of Methodism *numerically*, I will add nothing to the following statistical statement:

In 1792, there were 2 Preachers and 165 members; in 1800, there were 6 Preachers and 933 members; in 1810, there were 12 Preachers and 2,597 members; in 1820, there were 24 Preachers and 5,383 members; in 1830, there were 62 Preachers and 11,348 members; at present there are 101 Preach-ers and 15,453 members, besides regular and occasional hearers.

The progress of Methodism in a *civil* and *social* point of view is equal to its numerical increase. It has trampled over widespread and deep-rooted prejudices, by practical proofs that it is not a congeries[1] of enthusiastic impulses, but a consistent system of scriptural truth, rational experience, and sound morality.

Follow it in its progress from place to place, and the path of its *success* will be traced by a visible and essential improvement in piety and virtue, pub-lic order and individual happiness; in the enlargement of that kingdom which is "righteousness, and peace, and joy in the Holy Ghost."

Egerton Ryerson, *Wesleyan Methodism in Upper Canada* (Toronto, 1837), pp. 21-25.

[1] collection

8) **Roman Catholics in Upper Canada, Kingston, June 25, 1793**
Stuart to the Bishop of Nova Scotia

... After having got pretty well rid of the Methodists in my neighbourhood another Enemy makes its appearance, at the most distant part of the Settlement – the scotch Catholics near Johnstown have two Priests[1] among them, who, not content with the Toleration they enjoy of the public Exercises of their Religion amongst their own Sect, are assiduously employed in endeavouring to gain Proselytes[2] from those of our Communion. – In order to forward this Design, they disperse little Pamphlets through the protestant settlement. One of these was sent to me lately, by a Member of our Church requesting my advice. – It is Called *A Catholic's Reasons why he cannot become Protestant.* It contains nothing new, every argument in it has been fully answered in St.[K?] Jame's Time – I have collected and digested what I call, *A Protestant's Reasons why he cannot conform to the roman Catholic Religion,* and I intend to have a few copies of it printed and distributed in the lower Settlements by way of antidote. It is a mere collection from the Publications of James 2ᵈ Time, as I would not venture any Thing entirely my own; at least, till the effect of this has been tried.

Anglican Synod of Ontario, *Stuart Letters.*

9) **The Moravians**

In this neighbourhood [Niagara] live a set of religionists called *Moravians,* with long beards, originally from Germany; they emigrated to this place from Pennsylvania. They are a very innocent, inoffensive, and industrious people, that have many peculiarities in their manner of worship and mode of living, though of the Lutheran persuasion. In one settlement in that province they have all sorts of trades and manufactures, and have every thing in common. There is a large house or hall for the young women, apart, in which they work, and another for the young men in which they do the same. The sexes are never allowed to see one another. When a young man signifies a desire to marry, he and the first girl on the list are put into a private room together, and continue in it for an hour. If he agrees to marry her after this meeting, good and well; if not, he will not get another, and she is put the last on the list; so that all before her must go off before she gets any other offer. And though the parties had never seen one another before this meeting, which is rarely otherwise, they have no alternative, and must make up their minds and acquaintances in that short intercourse. If the parties are satisfied, and they marry, a house is built for them in the village where they live, and carry on business for the good of the community at large. There are as yet not above a score of

[1] The first Priest in Upper Canada was probably Alexander Mac-Donell, who came from Scotland and ministered to the Scots Highlanders of the Glengarry settlement until his death. The second Priest was probably Rev. Joachim MacDonell, who preached occasionally at Cornwall between 1784 and 1806.
[2] Converts from one religion to another.

them in this neighbourhood, but many more are expected; I have heard several people say that they would like them well as neighbours, and the Quakers are particularly fond of them on account of their mild and inoffensive dispositions.

P. Campbell, *op. cit.*, pp. 176-177.

10) **Morals in Upper Canada**

It is an idea entertained by the generality of the people of the United States, that the inhabitants of Canada are some of the worst people in the world, made up of rogues, murderers, and the like mean characters. However, the idea is entirely false. That there has some bad characters escaped from different parts of the United States to Canada, no one will deny; but these cannot be called the inhabitants, but only sojourners. But I may say, whether I am believed or not, that the main body of the people of Canada are peaceable, just, and generous in all their intercourse with each other, and strangers also; they are benevolent, being once poor themselves, they know how to feel for human want and human wo.[1] I have been acquainted with some of the inhabitants of almost every neighbourhood, and have found them to be nearly all alike, except those from England or Ireland. I have also attended a number of the courts of justice, and was surprised to see so little business done at them. The most of the inhabitants of the western or upper part of the province are from the states of New Jersey, Pennsylvania, and New York, and yet retain a considerable degree of that rectitude of conduct and conversation observed among the Quakers and Presbyterians in those states. There is hardly ever an instance of a person stealing in this province, not perhaps because all the inhabitants are too good, but partly from this cause, and partly because the penalty annexed to the crime is death; however, no one has been put to death in the province yet.

Smith, *op. cit.*, p. 15.

---

7.   Frontier Education

As students and teachers in Canadian schools, we are involved in the excitement, and some may add frenzy, of a rapidly changing educational system. We read of students' rights, teaching machines, ungraded schools, controversial government reports on education, equal educational opportunity for every child and hundreds of other new ideas and innovations. But have you, as a student, asked yourself why society is so concerned with your education?

[1] woe.

The following selections provide an opportunity to compare the present state of education with that which existed 150 years ago. Such a study poses the question how far have we progressed in education?

In cooperation with your teacher, suggest answers for the following questions about the educational system in which you are presently involved:

What are the educational objectives of your school?

How are your courses designed to meet these objectives?

How does society pay for your education? Why does it pay for your education?

Why does the law insist that eveyone must attend school to the age of sixteen?

How does one become a teacher?

Why are students protesting against our schools?

You will probably want to add to this list.

Once you have answered these questions, examine the following sources and compare your education to education before the war of 1812.

---

1. What was the purpose of education in pre-1812 Upper Canada?

2. How did the curriculum try to achieve these objectives?

3. Who went to school? Who paid for the support of education? Who received an education?

4. How did one become a teacher?

5. What were the strengths and weaknesses of education before 1812?

6. Compare education before 1812 to education in the present day.

7. Would Simcoe have approved of the direction taken by education before 1812?

1) Education at Cataraqui in 1786 to 1789
The First School

That he[1] applied to Gov[r] Hamilton[2] for the aid of Government to establish a School, and his Successor General Hope has erected a convenient Schoolhouse (which is almost finished) allowing a salary for an Assistant, till something permanent may be fixed; and he has committed the sole direction of the School to Mr. Stuart, and likewise the choice of an Assistant. That he opened the School in May last, and the number of Pupils is more than 30 at present. The Poor are taught gratis, and those who are able pay a moderate sum for tuition. When the School is properly arranged and has acquired the necessary

[1] John Stuart, in correspondence with his superiors, the Society of the Propagation of the Gospel, in London.

[2] Henry Hamilton was Administrator of British North America from 1782 to 1786.

reputation, he proposes to resign it to a capable assistant. He hopes the Society will approve his conduct in this instance of establishing a School, which bids fair to be so useful to the Loyalist Settlements in general.

Society for the Propagation of the Gospel, xxiv, 362-365.

2) Aims of education

1. There is a school, which was opened by myself in May 1786, ánd taught Gratis for 14 months. The present Master of it is Mr. Matthew Donovan, an Irishman. He teaches Spelling, Reading, Writing, Arithmetic, Mathematics, Latin & Greek.
2. He is diligent & competent to his Business; but has not been licensed according to Law.
3. He is attentive to the morals of the children, and instructs them in the Church Catechism.
. . . .
5. There are none besides the school in Kingston.
. . . .
[Endorsed] Send Oct. 2ᵈ 1789.

Anglican Synod of Ontario, *Stuart Letters.*

3) Education in Rural Areas

In a few years as the neighbourhood improved, school teaching was introduced by a few individuals whose bodily infirmities prevented them from hard manual weary labour.

At 7 years of age I was one of those who patronized Mrs. Cranahan, who opened a Sylvan Seminary for the young idea, from thence I went to Jonathan Clark's and then tried Thomas Morden, lastly William Faulkner, ...

You may suppose, that these gradations to Parnassus[1], was carried into effect because a large amount of knowledge could be obtained. Not so, for Dilworth's Spelling Book, and the New Testament, were the only two Books, possessed by these academiecians.

About 5 miles distant, was another teacher, whose name I do not recollect. After his days work was over in the woods, but principally in the Winter, he was ready to receive his pupils. This Evening School was for the express purpose of those in search of knowledge. My two elder Brothers availed themselves of this opportunity, and always went on snow shoes, which they deposited at the door, ready for their return – by moon-light and exciting occasions sometimes happened when the girls joined the Cavalcade. There the same process was gone thro' – Dilworth's Spelling Book, and the New Testament.

Those primeval days, I remember with great pleasure.

At 14, my education was finished, this was in 1806.

"Testimonial of Henry Rutlan," P.A.O., Merritt Papers, 40.

[1] Mountain in Greece, sacred in ancient times as a centre of poetic or artistic activity.

4) The inestimable advantages resulting from a well-educated and enlightened population, cannot be experienced in Canada for many years to come. The great mass of people are at present completely ignorant even of the rudiments of the most common learning. Very few can either read or write; and parents, who are ignorant themselves, possess so slight a relish for literature, and are so little acquainted with its advantages, that they feel scarcely any anxiety to have the minds of their children cultivated. . . .

Many circumstances concur to make it impracticable for the Canadians, even if they were capable, to educate their own children. In consequence of the difficulty of procuring labour, . . . , the farmer is not only compelled to devote himself entirely to the cultivation of his ground, but also to call in the aid of his sons, as soon as they are able to assist him. Boys of seven or eight years old are put to work, in Canada, and are kept at it during the remainder of their lives, – unless they acquire those habits of indolence which, I have before observed, are so general, as to preclude the devotion of much care and attention to any honest or equitable sort of trade. . . .

When the parent is sufficiently comfortable to dispense with the constant labour of his son, schools are perhaps too remote from his house to render them of any value to his children. Great are the advantages to be derived from a residence in the midst of a condensed and well-organized state of society; and numerous are the evils which result from a scanty population scattered over a wide and cheerless wilderness!

> E. A. Talbot, *Five Years' Residence in the Canadas* (London, 1824), Vol. II, pp. 116-119.

5) John Strachan[1] and the Cornwall Grammar School Objectives

Our first and most anxious care is to store the youthful mind with sound moral principles for it is a maxim with us that without knowing God, all knowledge is vain. Some boys make much greater progress in the acquisition of science than their companions – but to become a sincere Christian and a good member of Society is in every one's power. . . . We are aware that in paying so much attention to moral and religious improvement, we are acting contrary to the opinions of several late writers of considerable reputation who tell us that the greatest care should be taken to guard children from early prejudices. Those who are in favour of this method ought not to send their children here, for we are not disposed to admire the wisdom of these declaimers who advise us to teach the young no moral principles. . . . I shall never therefore despise the first dawnings of reason since they may be pointed to objects so invaluable.

> Kingston *Gazette*, September 3, 1811.

[1] John Strachan (1778-1867) came to Canada in 1799 to tutor the Children of Richard Cartwright. By 1803 he had become a deacon of the Anglican church and in 1839 he was appointed first Bishop of Toronto. As a key member of the Family Compact, he worked for the preservation of the Anglican church's position in all phases of Upper Canadian society.

6) Examinations

The first day was employed in examining the boys in their Classical and Scientific acquirements. . . .

The second day was taken up with debates, a variety of recitations, and exhibiting the mode of examining the classes in Civil and Natural History, Geography, &c. It was also usual on this day to recite one of Milman's or Miss Moore's Sacred Dramas. . . . But the most interesting business of the day was the opening of the Book of Merit, and the distribution of the prizes. This was done by the committee which had been appointed by the boys themselves to inspect the Registers and make out a list of the successful competitors. The names were read out by a member of the committee.

Kingston *Gazette*, September 3, 1811.

7) Student problems

Cornwall 14 June 1809

Dear Mother

"And sunk into oblivion"

Proper enough & very fit to be applied to myself. I am very badly off you know that very well "These tattered clothes my poverty bespeak". How true this is, if you cannot see it I can, for I am ragged & have nothing to put on. . . .

Send me my clothes quick – send me some money for the examination

Remain

Your aff: son

William Macaulay

P.A.O., Macauley Papers, MS. 78.

8) Accounts of District School at York

An Act[1] was passed into a Law by the Legislature of the Province of Upper Canada to establish Public Schools in each and every District of the Province.

His Excellency Governor Gore[2] through Major Halton his Secretary was pleased to appoint me[3] Teacher of the District School in York in the Home District. – The Letter dated the 16th April 1807.

On June 1st 1807 the District School was opened and the Pupils whose names follow were admitted. John Ridout – William A. Hamilton. Thomas G. Hamilton. George H. Detlor[4] George S. Boulton[5].

[1] The Public Schools Act of March 1807 provided for one grammar school to be established in each district, and further provide £100 per year to hire a teacher for each school.
[2] Lieutenant-Governor Gore arrived in Upper Canada in 1806, returned to England in 1812. After the war he once again served Upper Canada from 1815-1817.
[3] Rev. George Okill Stuart was the eldest son of the Rev. John Stuart.
[4] Detlor became a member of the House of Assembly.
[5] Boulton became a member of the House of Assembly and later the Legislative Council.

June 2d

Entered the District School on this day Robert Staunton[1]. William Staunton.

June 9th

Entered the District School on this day Angus McDonnell –

– 24th

Entered the District School on this day Hannah Jarvis and Eliza Anne Jarvis –

26

Entered the District School on Friday the 26th Mary Ridout –

30

Entered the District School on Tuesday the 30th. Anne McNabb and Hannah M. McNabb

July 1st. Wednesday

Entered the District School Alexander Hamilton & Wilson Hamilton

7th. Tuesday

Entered the District School Allan McNabb[2]

6th'

Entered the District School, Maria L. Jarvis

7th

Entered the District School William Jarvis.

Receipts

Received from Thomas Ridout Esqr. the Sum of eight Dollars for a Quarter's Tuition of John and Mary – $8

Received from Thomas Hamilton the Sum of twelve Dollars for the Tuition of Gilbert, William and Alexander Hamilton $12

Received from John Detlor the Sum of four dollars for a Quarter's Tuition of George H. Detlor in advance – $4

Received from William Jarvis Esqr. the Sum of sixteen Dollars for a Quarter's Tuition of Maria, Augusta, William and Hannah – $16

Received from Allan McNabb Esqr. the Sum of twelve Dollars for a Quarter's Tuition of Anne Allan and Hannah – $12

$64

T.P.L., G. O. Stuart Account Book.

9) **School Days at York**
   G. S. Jarvis[3] to Henry Scadding[4]

Cornwall 5 August 1869

. . . I am the George Jarvis named as one of the pupils of Dr. Stuarts school contemporaneous with the late Sir Allan McNab. . . . Sir Allan was the best speaker in the school, and was always ready for either a *frolic* or a *fight*.

[1] Staunton became editor of the *Upper Canada Gazette* and later Collector of Customs at Toronto.

[2] Sir Allan McNabb, famed for his military exploits in 1837 and his long career as a Conservative politician.

[3] George S. Jarvis served in the war of 1812 and later became a Judge.

[4] The first rector of Toronto's Church of the Holy Trinity.

The Dr was a very amiable man and very averse to use corporal punishment. When he found it necessary to have recourse to it he sent the delinquent out into his garden to cut the rod of course the smallest twig of the current bush was brought in. Sir Allan was sent out one occasion; and thinking he would escape by perpetrating a *good joke,* brought in a pretty large limb cut from an apple tree The Dr did not however see it in that light, and selecting the small part of it gave Sir Allan the most severe castigation I ever saw him inflict.

The boys were frequently in the habit of appropriating the Drs apples and he assured us that the first one detected in this act would be severely punished. On one occasion he detected Sir Allan eating something and pouncing upon him, just as he was putting the last morsel into his mouth, demanded "What are you eating McNab?" – Bread Sir! said the supposed delinquent, turning the half masticated contents of his mouth into his hand and presenting it for inspection. The Dr it is needless to say sat down rather in discomfiture at the giggle that ran round the school.

You have remarked that females were admitted to this School. Poor girls they were subjected to many annoyances and were unwittingly the cause of many battles between jealous boys. In one of these Sir Allan had a small piece of bone of the cheek at the lower part of the eye separated and it remained movable till the day of his death – This was a piece of my handy work. . . .

T.P.L., Scadding Papers, A103.

8.   Political Life before the War

By 1837, political life in Upper Canada had reached such an impasse that a significant segment of the population led by William Lyon Mackenzie resorted to armed rebellion against the government. At the time Sir Frances Bond Head was the Lieutenant Governor. The origins of this conflict, the so-called "Family Compact," can be traced back to 1791 when the constitution of Upper Canada, the Constitutional Act, was put into effect. Michael Smith has left us a good description of the operation of Upper Canada's government and its Constitution.

1. Construct a diagram to show the organization of Upper Canada's Government. What are the tasks of each part of the government?

2. While Smith states that the "people have got the means of guarding themselves," how might the will of the people be frustrated in this system?

3. Why does Smith make a point of indicating the nationalities of people in government? What is the significance of the high proportion of Americans in the Assembly and the relatively low proportion of Americans in other offices?

4. Patronage is the right to grant political offices or positions. Who controls patronage? What is the importance of controlling patronage?

1) Promiscuous Remarks on the Government – August 1812

The constitution, laws, and government of Upper Canada are much better than people, unacquainted with them, expect.

In the year 1791, the then called province of Quebec, was by an act of the British parliament divided into two separate provinces – to be called the province of Lower Canada, and the province of Upper Canada. By this act, a constitution was formed for each province, each in its nature calculated to suit the situation of their respective inhabitants – one being chiefly settled by the French, the other by the English.

The constitution put it out of the power of the British parliament to impose any taxes on the people, either upon their property or trade, but what was necessary for the regulation of commerce: but this should be disposed of by the legislature of the province, for the benefit of the same. The constitution also provides for the creation of a legislative council and a legislative assembly. The king also sends a governor who acts in the king's name. The members of the legislative council are selected by the king and governor jointly; these hold their seats during life if they do not forfeit it. The members of the legislative assembly are elected every 4th year by the freedom of the province. Any man of the age of 24, and who is worth property to the amount of 40s. a year, and has been in the province 7 years, may be elected a member of the legislative assembly, or vote for one. The making of laws for the welfare of the people is the business of the legislative assembly, must be assented to by the legislative council and governor, in the king's name, before they become laws, yet the legislative council, governor, British parliament or king, cannot make any laws for the people of Canada, "without the advice and consent of the legislative assembly."

From hence we see that the people have got the means of guarding themselves. About 12 years ago, the assembly passed an act dividing the province into districts or ridings, every one of which sends one member to parliament or the assembly. The number of members at present, August 1812, is 26, two thirds of which are natives of the United States; less than one third of the justices of the peace are Americans, the sheriffs are either Europeans or loyalists; the jury, according to the constitution, must be taken in rotation from each township, as their names stand on the assessment roll or list of names; of course the majority are always Americans. The majority of the courts . . . are Europeans; yet the proceedings of those courts are regulated by the acts of the assembly.

Smith, *op. cit.*, p. 17.

Political Dissent – 1807

Political life before 1812, when compared to the post war era, was rather tame. Despite occasional controversies, the government got on with the job of establishing necessary laws and statutes for the infant province of Upper Canada. Most people shared the attitude of Mrs. Catharine White who was too busy making a home in the bush to worry about "political strift, about Church Government or squabbling Municipal Councils. We left everything" she said "to our faithful Governor."[1]

This is, of course, not to suggest that political controversy did not exist before 1812. Perhaps the most significant and by far the most notorious opposition to the government of Upper Canada was led by a British-appointed judge, Robert Thorpe.

A controversial figure wherever he went, the Irish-born Thorpe used his courtroom as a sounding board for scathing indictments of the Lieutenant Governor, his Executive Council, and government supporters in the Legislative Council and House of Assembly. In the 1807 election, Thorpe won election to the Assembly where he tried to gain more financial power for the Assembly so that this body might have a larger share in the decision-making processes. Lieutenant-Governor Francis Gore eventually had Thorpe dismissed from office but the legacy of opposition started by Thorpe led to the first anti-government newspaper, *The Upper Canadian Guardian*, operated until 1812 by another Irishman Joseph Willcocks who sided with the Americans in the war and was eventually killed in battle.

Many historians trace the bitter party conflict between the Tories and Reformers in the 1820's and 1830's to the Thorpe incident.

From the following two sources, the first by Richard Cartwright, the second by Robert Thorpe, determine answers to the following questions.

1. If Cartwright reflects a Tory point of view and Thorpe a Reform view point, what principles or values are held by each group?

2. What foreign nations have influenced these views? Support your answers with evidence.

3. Why would Thorpe and Willcocks receive little support in Upper Canada?

2) Cartwright on the Thorpe Incident – Kingston, 14th March, 1807

Dear Sir, – Our Session of Parliament hath terminated in a manner the most desirable to the friends of good order, and the most mortifying to Mr. Thorpe, who has been completely foiled in his attempts to do mischief. The House of Assembly, by their late conduct, have made amends for the improprieties of the preceding session. Mr. Thorpe endeavoured to persuade them that the

[1] See pages 19-21.

duties levied under Acts of the British Parliament were at the disposal of the Provincial Legislature, ... He was here again left alone, notwithstanding his pathetic exclamation, that "if they gave up this they gave up their freedom," and his almost treasonable allusions to the American revolution, produced, as he said, by parliamentary taxation . . .

The removal of Mr. Thorpe has unquestionably relieved the Government of the Province from an active and indefatigable instrument of mischief; yet his friends here boast of his appointment at Sierra Leone as an unequivocal proof of the approbation of his conduct by His Majesty's Ministers; and this view of the subject is industriously obtruded upon the public, through the press of Mr. Wilcox,[1] his bosom friend and most zealous partizan.[2] The effects of his residence in this Province, however, will long be felt; for although we no longer hear the Government abused from the Bench by one of His Majesty's Judges, yet his example has given a degree of audacity to the factious that they would otherwise never have assumed. One of the most prominent characters among these is the before mentioned Mr. Wilcox, the printer, who, although once imprisoned by the House of Assembly for a libel on the majority of that House, and prosecuted, by the advice of the Attorney-General, for a most impudent libel on myself, still persists in attempting, by the grossest misrepresentations, to lessen the confidence of the people in the Government. In the prosecution for a libel, though its application was so pointed that its drift could not have been more clearly understood had my name been inserted at full length, he was acquitted; and such is the disposition of some of the people of this Province, that he has been returned a member of the House of Assembly for one of the Counties without opposition. It is, indeed, much to be regretted that while every demagogue has a probable chance of obtaining a seat in that House, the Government have it not in their power to return a single member.

C. E. Cartwright, *op. cit.*, pp. 131-136.

3) Thorpe Announces his Suspension

To the Freeholders of the East Riding of the County of York, and of the
    Counties of Durham and Simcoe.

Gentlemen.

When you called on me to represent you in Parliament, I answered that if you placed me in the House of Assembly I would discharge my duty faithfully; but I am now hurried to England, from the most insidious *misrepresentation* of my conduct having induced the Secretary of State to signify his Majesty's pleasure to suspend me from my Judicial Situation in this province. However the noble Lord at the head of the Colonial Department,[3] is actuated by the highest sentiments of honor, and the strictest principles of justice; therefore, truth, like the divine rod of Aaron, will quickly overcome the machinations of the Magicians.

Though wretched, even to agony, whilst under the slightest imputation,

[1] Willcocks.

[2] Enthusiastic supporter.

[3] Viscount Castlereagh.

yet your wellfare, your happiness and the prosperity of the province, shall engage my attention and animate my exertions. The objects dearest to me IN LIFE, I leave behind – that which is dearer THAN LIFE (MY HONOR) I hasten to defend; but if it pleases the Almighty to favor and protect me, my return shall be as rapid as my departure was unexpected.
Niagara, Nov. 2, 1807.

Niagara, *Upper Canada Guardian*, November 15, 1807.

9.   The War of 1812 in Upper Canada and the Common Man

The war of 1812 proved to be a turning point in Upper Canadian history. It demonstrated the loyalty of most Upper Canadians to Britain, proved Upper Canada's strategic position in North America and gave Upper Canadians an identity which was not entirely American or British. The causes and events of this war, while exciting and important, are readily available in most textbooks. Therefore, this unit will examine a question only fleetingly dealt with in standard sources; the effect of war upon the common man. The visitors, Michael Smith, an American writing in 1813 and John Howison, an Englishman writing shortly after the war have drawn interesting pictures of the war's impact on Upper Canada.

1. How did war affect the average Upper Canadian farmer? How did the war affect commerce?

2. What role did the "common man" play in the war? How did the war affect Upper Canadian morale?

3. How did the war affect Upper Canadian attitudes towards the United States?

1) An American's view of Upper Canada in 1813

Ever since the commencement of the war, there has been no collection of debts by law, in the upper part of the province, and towards the fall in no part; nor would one pay another. No person can get credit from any one to the amount of one dollar; nor can any one sell any of their property for any price, except provision of clothing; for those who have money, are determined to keep it for the last resort. No business is carried on by any person, except what is absolutely necessary for the time.

In the upper part of the province, all the schools are broken up, and no preaching is heard in all the land. All is gloomy – all is war and misery.

Upon the declaration of war, the governor laid an embargo on all the flour, wheat, and pork then in the province, destined for market, which was at a time when very little had left the province. The next harvest was truly bountiful, as also the crops of corn, buckwheat and peas; the most of which were gathered, except the buckwheat, which was on the ground when all the people were called away after the battle of Queenston; so that the people have a plenty of provision as yet (April, 1813). But, should the war continue, they must suffer, as not more than one half of the farmers, especially of the upper part of Canada, sowed any winter grain, because when they ought to have done it, they were called away to the lines. Although I say that the people in general have grain enough, yet some women are now suffering for bread, as their husbands are on the lines, and they and their children have no money nor credit, nor can they get any work to do.

Smith, *op cit.*, pp. 98-99.

2) John Howison's Impressions of the War's Impact on Upper Canada

The last American war forms an important era in the history of Upper Canada, and as such, it is continually referred to by the people, who, when alluding in a general way to the time at which any circumstance occurred, say that it happened before or after the war. The invasion of the Province excited no attention in Europe, or even in Britain, for at the time it took place we were engaged, in conjunction with the great continental powers, . . . However, the hostilities which took place in Upper Canada, although conducted on a small scale, were very interesting in their character, and would furnish excellent materials for a work such as is usually called a Campaign. A warfare carried on in a wild and wooded country, and with the assistance of Indian allies, is productive of incidents and events, which never occur in an open field of battle, nor during the re-encounter of regular troops.

The bravery of the Canadian militia, which was brilliantly conspicuous on many occasions, has neither been sufficiently known, nor duly appreciated, on the other side of the Atlantic . . . I am aware, that the gallantry of the native battalions of Upper Canada has been kept in the back-ground, by this want of generosity which prevails among the regular troops.

The last war was productive of most injurious consequences to the colony, and these have not been counterbalanced by a single advantage, except that the militia now feel a confidence in the efficiency of their arms, . . . Before the declaration of war took place, Upper Canada was in a state of progressive though slow improvement, and her inhabitants prudently attempted such exertions only as were proportioned to their means. Agriculture was pursued by all classes, and few thought of enriching themselves by any other occupation. But militia duty obliged them to abandon their farms, which were of course neglected, – the lands became waste, the cattle were carried away, and the buildings perhaps burnt by the enemy. However, the military establishments had brought such an influx of money into the country, that every one forgot his distresses, and thought himself on the high road to wealth, when he found he could sell any thing he possessed for double its real value, and have his pockets stuffed with army bills, as a recompense for some trifling service done to government. At this time, the abundance of circulating medium,[1] and the liberality with which it was expended, induced many people to bring large quantities of goods from Montreal, and retail stores soon became numerous in every part of the country. As the people continued to buy a great deal, and to pay for a great deal, the merchants willingly allowed them unlimited credit, erroneously supposing that their customers would always be able to discharge their debts, and that the temporary wealth of the Province would continue. But when peace was restored, when the troops were withdrawn, and all military operations suspended, the people soon perceived that a sad reverse awaited them. They found that the circulation of money gradually decreased, that they could no longer revel upon the bounty of a profuse government, and that they began to grow poorer every day; while the prospect of returning to their ravaged and uncultivated farms afforded but little consolation, as the spirit of industry had been extinguished by the lavish manner in which most of them had lived during the war. As a large portion of the live stock which the country contained had been carried away by the enemy, or consumed by our own troops, the farmers were obliged to purchase cattle from the Americans, and thus the country was still farther drained of much of the circulating specie,[2] and in a way too that produced no commercial advantages.

In course of time, the Montreal wholesale merchants began to urge their correspondents in the Upper Province for remittances, which many of the latter could not make; for, on applying to those whom they had formerly trusted to a large amount, they found that, with a few exceptions, they were alike unable and unwilling to discharge their debts. The country thus fell into a state of embarrassment, which continues to increase: most of the merchants have very large outstanding debts, which, if collected by means of suits, would ruin two-thirds of the farmers in the Province; and should the Montreal wholesale dealers have recourse to similar measures, many of their correspondents would become insolvent likewise. Both parties, therefore, judiciously temporize, being satisfied that it is, at present, the most advantageous policy they can pursue.

The war has had a most pernicious effect upon the morals of the people, which, I believe, were never very unexceptionable. The presence of a hostile army always enables those who are inclined, to commit excesses of every description with impunity; and example is more than usually contagious under such circumstances. Most of the American private soldiers were entirely destitue of moral principle, or any sense of decency, and often exhibited a wanton and unblushing profligacy, which in Europe would have received chastisement from the law. A good deal of this was communicated to the peasantry of Upper Canada, and the influence of the infection[3] is not yet entirely destroyed.

John Howison, *Sketches of Upper Canada* (Edinburgh: 1825), pp. 92-97.

[1] currency
[2] usually gold or silver coins, not paper money
[3] venereal disease

Topics for Further Inquiry

1. To what extent had Upper Canada, by 1812, followed Simcoe's blueprint?

2. Describe an imaginary trip from Montreal to Niagara in the year 1795.

3. As a merchant living at Kingston, write a letter to your Montreal agent in which you describe the prospects for commerce in the year 1795.

4. Compare life in rural Upper Canada before 1812 to that in an Upper Canadian town.

5. Write a brief autobiography of one of the following:
   1) a schoolboy(girl) in Upper Canada in 1800.
   2) a Methodist preacher in 1800.
   3) a Canadian militia man in 1813.
   4) a Kingston merchant in 1800.
   5) Robert Thorpe in 1807.

THREE

Rebellion in Upper Canada, *c.* 1815-1841

The rebellion in Upper Canada occurred in December 1837 because William Lyon Mackenzie led the people against a corrupt 'Family Compact'. This group of men governed Upper Canada and refused to give the people a say in government. The rebellion led to Lord Durham's report which brought democracy to Upper Canada.

Carefully examine this typical student description of the rebellion. From it, identify what is fact and what is the student's opinion. Certainly the date, December 1837, and the involvement of Mackenzie and a group called the "Family Compact" in the rebellion can be verified. But the student's judgements on the causes, the question of who was involved in the rebellion and the significance of the event, require further investigation. This unit then will provide readings which will give greater insight into the questions these raise. Before proceeding further, however, read the appropriate sections of your text in order to develop a list of the major events between 1815 and 1841. How does your text deal with the issues in question?

A Study of Causes

From your reading of the text you probably have realized that the student description which begins this unit has oversimplified the causes of the rebellion by blaming it on Mackenzie, a corrupt "Family Compact," and the people's desire for an increased role in government.

Professor C. G. Gustavson, in his very useful book *A Preface to History*, has provided us with a helpful guide to historical questions of causation.[1] Many of the following selections are therefore prefaced by one of Gustavson's analytical questions on causes.

From these it is hoped a greater understanding of the causes of the rebellion of 1837 will be gained, as well as the causes of an historical event.

[1] C. G. Gustavson, *A Preface to History* (Toronto: McGraw-Hill, 1955), pp. 53-64.

1.   What was the immediate cause for the event?

To pinpoint the precise instant at which an event begins is difficult and certainly subject to debate. Do the following two
sources, the first published in late November 1837, and the
second published December 7, 1837, two days after the first altercation, provide evidence to designate at least tentatively an
immediate cause?

1. What are the values and attitudes of Upper Canadians to which
   Mackenzie appeals? How do they differ from those expressed by
   Sir Francis Bond Head?

2. What propaganda devices do both authors use to convince their
   readers? What are the rewards offered to supporters by Mackenzie
   and by Head?

3. If these were the only sources available on the rebellion, what would
   you accept as fact? Why?

4. Why does Head call it an "unnatural Rebellion"?

5. What was the immediate cause for the event?

6. How accurate was the announcement contained in the third source?

1) William Lyon Mackenzie's call for Independence

Canadians! Do you love freedom? I know you do. Do you hate oppression?
Who dare deny it? Do you wish perpetual peace, and a government founded
upon the eternal heaven-born principle of the Lord Jesus Christ – a government
bound to enforce the law to do to each other as you would be done by? Then
buckle on your armour, and put down the villains who oppress and enslave
our country – . . . . You give a bounty for wolves' scalps. Why? because wolves
harrass you. The bounty you must pay for freedom (blessed word) is to give
the strength of your arms to put down tyranny at Toronto. One short hour will
deliver our country from the oppressor; and freedom in religion, peace and
tranquillity, equal laws and an improved country will be the prize. We con-
tend, that in all laws made, or to be made, every person shall be bound alike –
. . . . in the present struggle, we may be sure, that if we do not rise and put down
Head and his lawless myrmidons,[1] they will gather all the rogues and villains
in the Country together – arm them – and then deliver our farms, our families,
and our country to their brutality – to that it has come, we must put them down,
or they will utterly destroy this country. If we move now, as one man, to crush
the tyrant's power, to establish free institutions founded on God's law, we will
prosper, for He who commands the winds and waves will be with us – but if

[1] A mindless follower.

we are cowardly and mean-spirited, a woeful and a dark day is surely before us . . . .

Mark all those who join our enemies – act as spies for them – fight for them – or aid them – these men's properties shall pay the expense of the struggle – they are traitors to Canadian Freedom, and as such we will deal with them.

Mark my words Canadians! The struggle is begun – it might end in freedom – but timidity, cowardice, or tampering on our part, will only delay its close. We cannot be reconciled to Britain – we have humbled ourselves to the Pharoah of England, to the Ministers, and great people, and they will neither rule use justly nor let us go – we are determined never to rest until independence is ours – the prize is a splended one. A country larger than France or England, natural resources equal to our most boundless wishes – a government of equal laws – religion pure and undefiled – perpetual peace – education to all – millions of acres of lands for revenue – freedom from British tribute – free trade with all the world – but stop – I never could enumerate all the blessings attendant on independence!

Up then, brave Canadians! Get ready your rifles, and make short work of it; a connection with England would involve us in all her wars, undertaken for her own advantage, never for ours; with governors from England, we will have bribery at elections, corruption, villainy and perpetual discord in every township, but Independence would give us the means of enjoying many blessings. Our enemies in Toronto are in terror and dismay – they know their wickedness and dread our vengeance.

> Chas. Lindsey, *The Life and Times of William Lyon Mackenzie* (Toronto, 1862), pp. 358-362.

2) Proclamation

By His Excellency Sir Francis B. Head,
Baronet, Lieutenant Governor of Upper Canada, &c. &c.

To the Queen's Faithful Subjects in Upper Canada.
In a time of profound peace, while every one was quietly following his occupations, feeling secure under the protection of our Laws, a band of Rebels, instigated by a few malignant and disloyal men, has had the wickedness and audacity to assemble with Arms, and to attack and Murder the Queen's Subjects on the Highway – to Burn and Destroy their Property – to Rob the Public Mails – and to threaten to Plunder the Banks – and to Fire the City of Toronto.

Brave and Loyal People of Upper Canada, we have been long suffering from the acts and endeavours of concealed Traitors, but this is the first time that Rebellion has dared to shew itself openly in the land, in the absence of invasion by any Foreign Enemy.

Let every man do his duty now, and it will be the last time that we or our children shall see our lives or properties endangered, or the Authority of our Gracious Queen insulted by such treachery and ungrateful men. MILITIA-MEN OF UPPER CANADA, no Country has ever shewn a finer example of Loyalty and

Spirit than YOU have given upon this sudden call of Duty. Young and old of all ranks, are flocking to the Standard of their Country. What has taken place will enable our Queen to know Her Friends from Her Enemies — Public Enemy is never so dangerous as a concealed Traitor — and now my friends let us complete well what is begun — let us now return to our rest till Treason and Traitors are revealed to the light of day, and rendered harmless throughout the land.

Be vigilant, patient and active, — leave punishment to the Laws, — our first object is, to arrest and secure all those who have been guilty of Rebellion, Murder and Robbery. — And to aid us in this, a Reward is hereby offered of

One Thousand Pounds,

to any one who will apprehend, and deliver up to Justice, *William Lyon Mackenzie* — and *Five Hundred Pounds* to any one who will apprehend, and deliver up to Justice, *David Gibson*[1] — or *Samuel Lount*[2] — or *Jesse Lloyd*[3] — or *Silas Fletcher*[4] — and the same reward, and a free pardon, will be given to any accomplices who will render this public service, except he or they shall have committed, in his own person, the crime of Murder or Arson.

And all, but the Leaders above-named, who have been seduced to join in this unnatural Rebellion, are hereby called to return to their duty to their Sovereign — to obey the Laws — and to live henceforward as good and faithful Subjects — and they will find the Government of their Queen as indulgent as it is just.

GOD SAVE THE QUEEN.

Thursday, 3 o'clock, P.M.
7th December.

Upper Canada Gazette, December 7, 1837.

3) Result of Rebellion

The Party of Rebels, under their Chief Leaders, is wholly dispersed, and flying before the Loyal Militia. The only thing that remains to be done, is to find them, and arrest them.

Upper Canada Gazette, December 7, 1837.

[1] An Assemblyman and member of Mackenzie's Committee on Grievences, who allowed his house on Yonge Street to be used as a rebel meeting centre.

[2] Born in Pennsylvania in 1791, and ultimately executed for his part in the rebellion.

[3] Born in Pennsylvania in 1786, he was a close associate of Mackenzie and helped plan the rebellion.

[4] Born in New Hampshire in 1780, another of Mackenzie's close associates.

2.

Was there a background of agitation for the principles which triumphed during the episode?

Many students, once the immediate cause was identified, would consider their task complete. The historically-minded student, however, would be compelled by his natural curiosity to probe further into the roots of the problem. It is evident, for instance, from previous readings in this section, that the major issue was the conflict between independence for Upper Canada and loyalty to the British Empire. The origins of this issue are, of course, deep and complex and certainly not spelled out as clearly as in 1837. But the career of Robert Gourlay, in Upper Canada from 1817 until the government of the Province expelled him in 1819, reflects the principles which conflicted in 1837.

Robert Gourlay, a Scotsman, came to Upper Canada two years after the war with the United States had ended. Upon his arrival, he found a colony, particularly in official circles, which was violently anti-American in attitude and enthusiastically pro-British. To ensure the continuance of Upper Canada as a British colony and to prevent its Americanization and eventual independence, the government of Upper Canada had passed laws to restrict American settlement in Upper Canada and took steps to encourage settlers from the British Isles. It was under these circumstances that Gourlay requested and was granted permission to have a list of 31 questions on the condition of Upper Canada printed in the government's newspaper the *Upper Canada Gazette*. His stated purpose was to gain information in order to publish "A Statistical Account of Upper Canada" which would then be used to encourage British settlers to come to Upper Canada. All but question 31 were non-controversial in nature. This last question, which asked: "What in your opinion retards the improvement of your township in particular or the province in general, and what would most contribute to the same?" virtually invited criticism of the government of Upper Canada.

1. What principle triumphed in 1837 according to the third document?

2. On what grounds did Gourlay criticize the government? How did the government react to his criticism?

3. How did Gourlay communicate his views?

4. Was Gourlay a responsible critic of government or an irresponsible agitator?

5. Compare the principles involved in Gourlay's conflict with Administrator Smith and Lieutenant-Governor Maitland to those of Mackenzie's rebellion against Head's government.

1) Address by Robert Gourlay

To the Resident Land Owners of Upper Canada.

Queenston, Feb., 1818

Gentlemen,

I did myself the honour of addressing you through the medium of the Upper Canada *Gazette* of the 30th of October last, and my address has been since widely circulated over the Province by various other Channels. Its object was to gain the most authentic intelligence concerning this Country for the information of our fellow-subjects and Government at home. . . .

Since then three months have passed away. In this time I have travelled more than a thousand miles over the Province. I have conversed with hundreds of the most respectable people. I have gravely and deliberately considered what I have heard and seen. I have changed my mind; and, most unwillingly must change my course of proceeding. This country, I am now convinced, cannot be saved from ruin by temporizing measures nor by the efforts and reasoning of any individual – if it is to be saved reason and fact must speedily be urged before the Throne of our Sovereign by the united voice of a loyal and determined people – if it is to be saved your Parliament now assembled must be held up to its duty by the strength and spirits of its constituents. . . .

In my humble opinion, Gentlemen, there ought to be an immediate Parliamentary enquiry into the state of this Province, and a Commission appointed to proceed to England with the result of such enquiry.

> E. A. Cruikshank, "The Government of Upper Canada and Robert Gourlay: Illustrative Documents, 1814-1821," *Ontario Historical Society Papers and Records* (1926), pp. 124-125.

2) From Robert Gourlay to Sir Henry Torrens[1]

Queenston, Upper Canada,

My Dear Sir   Feby. 7th, 1818

. . . .

You know that I am free in the expression of my opinions – probably more so than you think right; but I believe you never doubted my honour or good intentions and I never pledged them more solemnly than now.

The Canadas have hitherto only been a Bill of Expence to Britain. Managed on a liberal footing I am persuaded they might not only pay all expenses incurred but yield to Government a considerable revenue.

Since I last wrote I have travelled upwards of a thousand miles through this Province. Everywhere I found the people well disposed to Government, but quite disappointed & dispirited with occurrences which might have been prevented. They see the property of their neighbours in the United States advancing in value while theirs is on the decline; they see everything in motion there, while all is here at a stand: they see the claims of Americans who suffered by the War attended to & on the eve of being paid, while theirs are almost despaired of. From where I now write I overlook the ruins of the house of the

[1] British Under Secretary of State for War.

late Honble Robert Hamilton[1] my wife's uncle. This house was the best in the Province and for many years afforded the most liberal welcome to every Gentleman who visited the Country. It was entailed on his son with provision to continue in it the hospitality of its founder; but in the war it was seized by the Military for barracks; and in their possession was burned down. It is now the fourth year without a farthing being paid in recompense for the loss. . . .

I am with respect & esteem
Yours etc.
Robert Gourlay

Ibid., p. 132.

3) From Samuel Smith[2] to Earl Bathurst[3]

Upper Canada,

R. 21st April.   York, 23rd February, 1818

My Lord,

Interested Individuals however, who by an inconsiderate policy had been permitted to purchase large Tracts, to the extent of 100,000 Acres from the Grand River Indians, were affected by this regulation, which prevented the sale of their Lands to these strangers, and they had influence enough to bring this subject before the Legislature in the Offensive shape which induced Mr. Gore to prorogue the Assembly.

They have now found a support out of the House in a reformer from the United Kingdom, whose declarations in the Provincial Gazettes are not less inflammatory amongst an ignorant population from the want of Truth, reason and decorum.

This man, Robert Gourlay, one of whose lucubrations[4] I have the honour to enclose has no property or residence in the Colony, and is only known as a relative to Mr. Dickson, the proprietor of a Grand River Township.

My Lord, this man's significance is no security against the mischief he may generate. . . .

I have the honour to be
My Lord, &c.
Saml. Smith
Administrator.

Ibid., pp. 133-134.

[1] A merchant at Niagara, a large landowner and a close business associate of Richard Cartwright. He died in 1809.

[2] Administrator of Upper Canada when Sir Francis Gore returned to England in 1817. He remained in this office until Sir Peregrine Maitland took office as Lieutenant-Governor in August of 1818.

[3] British Secretary of State for War and the Colonies, 1812-1827.

[4] An overly-elaborate literary work.

4) Maitland[1] to Goulbourn[2]

22nd July 1819

I have had no little trouble from the indefatigable labours of this Mr. Gourlay, who first gave out that he was commissioned by H. Majesties Government to report upon the state of the Province. The fellow in a Province like this was superlatively mischievous as long as he had the only two papers that are read completely in his interest, for the Government paper, it was said, out of delicacy, took no part. The liberty of the Press is however now established and he was sinking into significance when two Legislative Councillors on the 44th of the King perplexed me by taking him up and ordering him out of the Province. He would not go and they have put him in Gaol. I am afraid this will give him a new interest for a short time, but I trust under the blessing of the Lord, that all will end peaceably. I have no sort of apprehension and intend to let the law take its course – I had intended to have pursued different measures, but that which I would not have done, it would on many accounts be imprudent to undo.

Ibid., p. 97.

5) Gourlay Jailed, July 1819
John Goldie's Diary

The only building worthy of particular notice is the Jail, which stands about a quarter of a mile out of the town. It is a large two-storey house of brick, very handsome, and is considered to be the finest building in Canada. At present it holds within its walls the celebrated Gourley. A few of the Niagara newspapers that I have seen are nearly filled with his writings and those of his opponents. However, I believe that he generally remains last on the field, which is commonly considered a proof of victory. One of his papers which was of great length, I read, and, from the sentiments it contains, I cannot think that he is so dangerous a character as the men in power would have people believe. He is very free in giving his opinion concerning the character of the Governors, and I suspect his greatest fault is speaking too many truths, which are not thought to be seasonable or agreeable. He asserts positively that the Duke of Richmond[3] came to Canada solely for the purpose of making money, and that Sir P. Maitland made a runaway marriage with a daughter of the Duke's in France, but that peace was made through the mediation of the Duke of Wellington[4] under whom Sir Peregrine was serving at that time; and that this connection elevated him greatly and eventually made him Governor of Upper Canada, (p. 22).

Ibid., p. 99.

[1] Sir Peregrine Maitland was Lieutenant-Governor of Upper Canada from 1818 to 1828.

[2] Henry Goulbourn (1784-1856), English statesman and commissioner in the negotiations for peace with the United States in 1814, held a variety of important positions in the British government.

[3] Governor in Chief of the Canadas from 1818 until his death in 1819.

[4] Hero of the battle of Waterloo, and Prime Minister of Great Britain from 1828 to 1830.

3.   Were personalities involved on either side whose
strengths and weaknesses may have helped to
determine the outcome of the struggle?

An interesting historical exercise is the "if" game. How might
the course of history have been altered if Lee Harvey Oswald
had missed, or if Lenin's assassin had succeeded, if Ted Kennedy
had turned left instead of right, if Christ had died in infancy, or
if William Lyon Mackenzie had never left Scotland? Such questions lead to the debate of the role of the individual in history.
Can individuals really determine the course of history, or are
they swept along by a tide of events and circumstances beyond
their control? Professor Sidney Hook[1] has categorized "event-
making men" as those individuals, who through their special
genius, redirect the course of history. "Eventful men" are those
who prove to be the right or wrong individuals at the right or
wrong time and find themselves shaped by historical forces. From
the documentary evidence presented in Part Three, consider if
William Lyon Mackenzie fits either description.

In 1837, many individuals were involved in the events of
the rebellion, Lieutenant Governor Head, John Strachan, Egerton
Ryerson,[2] Robert Baldwin,[3] to name only a few. But certainly the
most colourful and controversial was Mackenzie.

Most of the selections used so far have emphasized the value
of primary sources. The following selections, which concern
Mackenzie, will examine historiography, the writing of history.

1. On what bases do the authors of the first two documents criticize
   Mackenzie?

2. Why might Ryerson's testimony be of questionable value?

3. How do the authors of documents three and four answer the criti-
   cisms raised in the first two items? What arguments do the former
   suggest to show Mackenzie in a more positive light?

4. Which argument is most convincing? Why? What further research
   do you feel is necessary to make a sound evaluation?

1) Mackenzie, the Agitator

The correct estimate of Mackenzie would be that he was first and last an
agitator. He cannot be credited with leadership in any of the more prominent
issues before 1837. That leadership was assumed by Gourlay, Ryerson, the

[1] Sidney Hook, *Hero in History* (Boston: Beacon Press, 1955).
[2] A Methodist minister, who gained fame for his opposition to Strachan
and the Church of England. In 1836, he broke with Mackenzie
because of Mackenzie's radical policies.
[3] See note on page 90.

Bidwells,[1] Robert Baldwin, and lesser figures. But Mackenzie was adept at seizing other people's ideas and promulgating them as his own, though his great weakness was that he could place evils in no order of importance. Ryerson said of him that "every evil which he discerned was in his estimation truly an evil and all evils were about of equal magnitude. . . . He felt a longing desire to right the wrongs which he saw everywhere around him. This, there-fore, constituted, as he believed his mission as a public man in Canada."

> F. Landon, "The Common Man in the Era of the Rebellion of Upper Canada," *Canadian Historical Association Report*, 1937, p. 77.

2) William Lyon Mackenzie is a prominent figure in Canadian history. The notoriety which he naturally acquired as leader of a rebellion in 1837 has stamped his importance on the minds of posterity. Moreover, Mackenzie was the type of man who thirsts for publicity, and who pushes himself forward on every possible occasion. An incessant writer, he has left ample evidence of his multifarious activities. As a result he has been accorded a pre-eminence in the period prior to 1837 which needs qualification. The name of Gourlay its attached to the agitation against the land policy, that of the Bidwells to the alien question,[2] that of Egerton Ryerson to the clergy reserves, that of the Baldwins to responsible government, but Mackenzie never succeeded in taking the leadership on any prominent issue. Nor had he throughout life a decided policy. At any one moment from 1820 to 1837 his writings were but the reflec-tion of the miscellaneous complaints which happened to be prevalent. Before 1828 he was known only as the obscure editor of one of several radical news-papers, . . . In 1828 he entered the assembly and made himself conspicuous as an agitator, but it was Marshall Spring Bidwell, not Mackenzie, who was elected speaker by the reformers, both in 1828 and 1835, and the speakership was then the only official position of party eminence attainable. . . . Bidwell's ability as a lawyer and a politician was universally acknowledged, and as an opponent he was respected, whereas Mackenzie was regarded merely as a troublesome agitator and a demagogue. . . . Mackenzie was not a thinker but a fighter. His task was to popularize other people's ideas. The only originality which he ever exhibited was a certain critical ability in finance, . . . As an agitator, however, and a scathing opponent of the existing government, root and branch, his energy after 1828 was indefatigable and his influence pre-eminent. . . .

> A. Dunham, *Political Unrest in Upper Canada* (McClelland and Stewart, 1963), pp. 105-106.

[1] Barnabas Bidwell, American born and educated, was a fugitive from American justice, who gained a seat in the Upper Canadian legisla-ture where he led the fight against government land policies. He was shortly expelled from the legislature because of his moral character. Marshall Spring Bidwell, son of Barnabas, was also born in the United States. A member of the legislative assembly from 1825 to 1836, he took a leading role in criticizing government policies. He opposed Mackenzie's rebellion and took no part in it.

[2] The Bidwells opposed the government's policy of restricting Ameri-can immigration after the war of 1812.

3) Mackenzie the Constructive Critic

Indeed, a superficial examination may easily leave the impression that intellectually Mackenzie was a mere jumble of contradictions, and it would be easy to make out a case to this effect, by testing him on the basis of isolated statements torn from their context, or by comparing his views at different periods of his career. But closer study reveals an inner unity and coherence, a unity based less on political remedies than on political attitudes. At heart Mackenzie always remained a Puritan[1] with a mission. . . . early training left a puritan cast of mind which became more rigid with age. This puritan view of life Mackenzie transferred to politics. The fundamental tenet of his political faith was that government was a trust to be administered on behalf of the governed. . . . Any deviation by a public man from the straight and narrow path of disinterested public service, any abuse of public office for private advantage, high salaries and exorbitant fees, any undue private gain from public measures, were venal acts which should be denounced and exposed for the public good. Above all, the people's representative must not only do no evil, he must avoid the appearance of evil be refusing public office or association with private interests which might benefit from public policy. There could be no compromise with Satan. . . .

Superficially Mackenzie's ideas changed radically, sometimes with almost breath-taking suddenness, partly because he was ever ready to admit errors of judgment. Yet there is throughout a development about this central theme of government as a trust.

> R. A. MacKay, "The Political Ideas of William Lyon Mackenzie," *The Canadian Journal of Economics and Political Science*, Vol. III, February, 1937, p. 3.

4) . . . It has been said that Mackenzie never succeeded in taking the leadership on any prominent issue nor had he throughout his life a "decided" policy.

Mackenzie agitated on many subjects and it has to be admitted that he changed his mind on some of them, but it is unfair to dismiss him as a chattering agitator without any overall conceptions and unable to make good use of the facts he unearthed. He came to see that Upper Canada did not in reality enjoy the image and transcript of the British constitution and that, in any event, British political institutions could not be successfully transplanted unmodified to a frontier society with a very different social structure. . . . In his opinion the real wealth of the country was being created by the labour of the settlers and he wanted to safeguard it for them, both in the form of improved properties of their own and in increasingly valuable public land.

. . . . His ideal society was one which secured for every man the greatest possible quantity of the product of his own labour, and denied existence to any privileged political, religious, or economic interests, who might steal from him.

Mackenzie's guiding idea was that the province should be a community

[1] In this case, Puritan describes Mackenzie's strict and uncompromising religious and moral beliefs.

of simple living, hard working, frugal, independent farmers served by honest merchants, craftsmen, small manufacturers, township schools, an honest legislature, and a free press; in short an educated and largely agrarian democracy.

> L. F. Gates, "The Decided Policy of William Lyon Mackenzie," *Canadian Historical Review*, XL (1959), pp. 186-187.

4. Were any new and potent ideas stimulating the loyalty of a considerable number of people?

Why are boys now wearing long hair and girls mini-skirts? Why are students throughout the world participating in mass protests? Why is there a war in Vietnam? Have you ever asked yourself any of these questions? If you have, you probably concluded that each issue reflected new and conflicting ideas.

Carl Gustavson has defined ideas as "the threads which bind the minds of men together sufficiently for joint action to occur."[1] Our task then is to identify, define, and evaluate the impact of those threads which contributed to the rebellions of 1837.

1. Compare Mackenzie's Declaration of Independence to the American Declaration. (This will be available in most texts on American history.) What was Jacksonian Democracy? By re-examining Mackenzie's Declaration, suggest how Jacksonian Democracy influenced Upper Canada.

2. How does Robert Baldwin, a moderate reformer, propose to alter the system of government? Why would Britain find Baldwin's approach more acceptable than Mackenzie's proposals for governmental change?

1) Mackenzie's Declaration of Independence

We have planted the Standard of Liberty in Canada, for the attainment of the following objects:

Perpetual Peace, founded on a government of equal rights to all, secured by a written constitution, sanctioned by yourselves in a convention to be called as early as circumstances will permit.

Civil and Religious Liberty, in its fullest extent, that in all laws made, or to be made, every person be bound alike – . . . .

The Abolition of Hereditary Honors, . . . , and of hosts of pensioners who devour our substance.

[1] Gustavson, *op. cit.*, p. 153.

A Legislature, composed of a Senate and Assembly chosen by the people.

An Executive, to be composed of a Governor and other officers elected by the public voice.

A Judiciary, to be chosen by the Govenor and Senate, and composed of the most learned, honorable, and trustworthy, of our citizens. The laws to be rendered cheap and expeditious.

A Free Trial by Jury – Sheriffs chosen by you, and not to hold office, as now, at the pleasure of our tyrants. The freedom of the press. Alas for it, now! The free presses in the Canadas are trampled down by the hand of arbitrary power.

The Vote by Ballot – free and peaceful township elections.

. . . .

Freedom of Trade – every man to be allowed to buy at the cheapest market, and sell at the dearest.

No man to be compelled to give military service, unless it be his choice.

Ample funds to be reserved from the vast natural resources of our country to secure the blessings of education to every citizen.

A frugal and economical Government, in order that the people may be prosperous and free from difficulty.

An end forever to the wearisome prayers, supplications, and mockeries attendant upon our connection with the lordlings of the Colonial Office, Downing Street, London.

. . . .

For the attainment of these important objects, the patriots now in arms under the Standard of Liberty, on *Navy Island, U. C.*, have established a Provisional Government of which the members are as follows, (with two other distinguished gentlemen, whose names there are powerful reasons for withholding from public view,) viz: William L. Mackenzie, Chairman pro-tem.

Lindsey, *op. cit.*, pp. 363-365.

2) **Robert Baldwin[1] to Lord Glenelg[2]**

I now come to the consideration of the fourth remedy, which consists of nothing more than having the provincial Government as far as regards the internal affairs of the Province, conducted by the Lieutenant Governor . . . with the advice and assistance of the Executive Council, acting as a Provincial Cabinet, and composed of Men possessed of the public confidence, whose opinions and policy would be in harmony with the opinions and policy of the Representatives of the People. This, . . . , I look upon not only as an efficient remedy, but as

[1] Son of Dr. W. W. Baldwin a noted opponent of the Family Compact, Robert Baldwin was a leading moderate. On one hand he criticized the Family Compact, but on the other hand he objected to Mackenzie's radical plans. Baldwin's political life is characterized by his unswerving fight for responsible government, a fight ultimately won in 1849.

[2] British Colonial Secretary.

the only efficient one that can be applied to the evils under which the Province is at present suffering.

> W. P. M. Kennedy, ed., *Statutes, Treaties and Documents of the Canadian Constitution, 1713-1929* (Toronto: Oxford University Press, 1930), pp. 338-339.

5.   How did economic groups line up on the issue?

One of Canada's foremost historians, D. G. Creighton, has argued with reference to the 1837 rebellion that "the conflict in the Canadas was in large measure a social conflict which grew naturally out of the disturbed economy of the St. Lawrence."[1] The purpose of this section is two-fold. The first is to analyze and evaluate Creighton's hypothesis, and the second to examine the social and economic structure of Upper Canada from 1815 to 1837, in order to determine the changes which took place after the war of 1812.

1. With American immigration cut off after 1812, what changes took place in the immigrants arriving in Upper Canada.

2. Why would the post-war immigrants find more difficulty in adjusting to life in Upper Canada than those who came to Canada before 1812?

3. How did the frontier affect the attitudes of immigrants from Europe?

4. Account for the drinking and gambling of male immigrants and the unhappiness of women in Upper Canada.

5. Why might frontier living contribute to rebellion?

6. Why might the new immigrants be more loyal than those who came before the war?

1) Frontier influence

It is very remarkable, that although the present population of this fine Province is composed of emigrants from almost every European nation, and from every state of North America, there should be so little difference in their manners, customs, and habits of life. Germans, Hollanders, French English, Scotch, and Irish, after a few years' residence in Canada, forget their national customs and

[1] D. G. Creighton, "The Economic Background of the Rebellions of 1837," *Canadian Journal of Economic and Political Science* (1931), p. 323.

peculiarities, and become, in almost every particular, entirely assimilated to the people of America.

These emigrants, having generally been of the lowest class of society in their respective countries, – and consequently mere cyphers except in their own immediate sphere, – as soon as they arrive in Canada, begin to assume an appearance of importance, and to be quite ashamed of their former unassuming manners and native customs. The most absurd notions of equality and independence take instant possession of their . . . minds. As they travel through the Province and mingle with its inhabitants, they hear the dialects and peculiarities of their respective nations . . . ridiculed, while those of America, . . . , are invariably defended. . . . The first, and, as they conceive it, the most essential study in which they can engage in this new state of existence, is therefore to imitate everything American; and so successful are they in their endeavours to copy the example of those by whom they are surrounded, that, before they have spent a single season in the Province, they exhibit the most ludicrous specimens of ignorance and affectation that this or any other country can produce. Not a single trace of native simplicity or of native manners remains. . . . They are indefatigable in acquiring a knowledge of the Rights of Man, the First Principles of Equality, and the True Nature of Independence, and, in a word, of every thing which characterises an American; and thus they quickly become divested of common manners, and common civility, and not infrequently of common honesty too.

> E. A. Talbot, *Five Years' Residence in the Canadas* (London, 1824), Vol. II, pp. 9-11.

2) Immigrant Problems

The greater portion of British emigrants, arriving in Canada without funds and the most exalted ideas of the value and productiveness of land, purchase extensively on credit, and take up their abode in the midst of the forest, with the proudest feelings of independence, and in the confident hope of meeting their engagements, and becoming fine gentlemen at the end of a few years. Every thing goes on well for a short time. A log-house is erected with the assistance of old settlers, and the clearing of forest is commenced. Credit is obtained at a neighbouring store, and at length it is found necessary to work a day or two in the week for hire to obtain food for the familly. The few garden stuffs and field crops, grown the first year, produce little for want of a free circulation of air, and the imperfect manner in which they had been sown. Should fever and ague now visit the emigrant, which is frequently the case, the situation of himself and family, enfeebled by disease, is truly wretched. Hope, is however, still bright, and he struggles through the second year, with better crops and prospects than the preceding one. The third year brings him good crops, which furnish a supply of food for his establishment. During this period he has led a life of toil and privation, being poorly fed and most uncomfortably lodged. But the thought of owning so many fair acres has been a never-failing source of joy and sweetener of life. On arrival of the fourth harvest, he is reminded by the storekeeper to pay his account with cash, or discharge part of it with his disposable produce, for which he gets a very small price. He is also informed that the purchase-money of the land has been accumulating with interest. The phantom of prosperity, conjured up by his imagination, is now dispelled, and, on calmly looking into his affairs, he finds himself poorer than when he commenced operations. Disappointment preys on his spirits, and the aid of whisky is perhaps sought to raise them. The hopelessness of his situation render him indolent and immoral. The land ultimately reverts to the former proprietor, or a new purchaser is found.

> Patrick Shirreff, *A Tour through North America* (Edinburgh, 1835), pp. 362-363.

3) Social Pressures: male

The Canadians are very much addicted to drinking; and, on account of the cheapness of liquor, are very frequently under its influence. Card-playing, horse-racing, wrestling, and dancing, are their favourite amusements; and as the jingle of a dollar is a [rare] sound in the ear of a Canadian, . . . , their bets are usually made in stock, and are sometimes exceedingly extravagant. The fate of a cow, a yoke of oxen, or a pair of horses, is often determined by the colour of a card; and an hour's gambling has deprived many a Canadian farmer of the hard-earned fruits of twenty years' industry.

> E. A. Talbot, *op. cit.*, vol. II, pp. 57-58.

4) Social Pressures: female

. . . women that come hither give way to melancholy regrets, and destroy the harmony of their fireside, and deaden the energies of their husbands and brothers by constant and useless repining[1]. . . .

One poor woman that was lamenting the miseries of this country was obliged to acknowledge that her prospects were far better than they ever had or could have been at home. What, then, was the cause of her continual regret and discontent, I could hardly forbear smiling when she replied, "She could not go to shop of a Saturday night to lay out her husband's earnings, and have a little chat with her naibors,[2] while the shopman was serving the customers, – for why, there were no shops in the bush, and she was just dead-alive. If Mrs. Such-a-one" (with whom, by the way, she was always quarrelling when they lived under the same roof) "was near her she might not feel quite so lonesome." And so for the sake of a dish of gossip, while lolling her elbows on the counter of a village-shop, this foolish woman would have forgone the advantages, real solid advantages, of having land and cattle, and poultry and food, and firing and clothing, and all for a few years' hard work, which, her husband wisely observed, must have been exerted at home, with no other end in view than an old age of poverty or a refuge from starvation in a parish workhouse.

[1] complaining
[2] neighbours

The female of the middling or better class, in her turn, pines for the society of the circle of friends she has quitted, probably for ever. She sighs for those little domestic comforts, that display of the refinements and elegancies of life, that she has been accustomed to see around her. She has little time now for those pursuits that were even her business as well as amusement.

> Catharine Parr Traill, *The Backwoods of Canada* (Toronto: Mc-
> Clelland and Stewart, 1929), pp. 190-191.

6.   Changes in Town Life

1. By comparing Francis Jackson's description of York in 1831 to the description of York on pages 54-56, determine the changes which had taken place in the physical and social structures of York.

2. By examining the first three sources, determine some of the problems faced by citizens of a town.

3. What evidence indicates the existence of social classes in towns?

4. By examining the second document, state society's attitude toward social welfare.

5. How might changing conditions in towns contribute to rebellion?

1) A Letter from Francis Jackson[1]

. . . I will now give you a brief account of the town of York: – It is a modern built place. Thirty years ago it was a forest, and 7 years since it was only a small village; it is now a flourishing place, and laid out for a large town. The streets are straight and wide. . . . It is full of respectable inhabitants of every description, and their shops are well stocked with all kinds of goods, . . . There were 300 houses built last year. This year I suppose there are more than 400 built and building. They are now building a parliament house, and a large college. Next summer they are going to build a church and a university. The principal buildings are the jail, court-house, bank and hospital. The houses are built, some of brick and some of wood. . . . We had William the Fourth proclaimed here in grand style. – The governor and the officers of the 71st regiment with the band, and the gentlemen both in the town and county, went in procession in their coaches, gigs, &c. the band playing "God save the King," and "Rule Britannia" . . . This town is inhabited by people from different nations, such as English, Irish, Scotch, & Dutch, with a few Canadians & Yankees, but the English have the pre-eminence, and are the most predominant. We have people from all parts of England, with a great many from Yorkshire. This place resembles England the most of any place I have seen. As for the manners and

[1] A tailor who lived on Church Street.

customs of the people, I find no difference between them and the people of the old country, only in minor points, and the different modes of religion are the same as in England. We have Methodists, Ranters, Baptists, Quakers, Catholics and Protestants; but the English church is the established religion, I will now give you some statement of wages, the price of provisions, land, &c. Bricklayers have 7s. 6d. per day.. Smiths have 7s. 6d. for setting four shoes on a horse. Joiners, 6s. per day. Tailors have £1 5s. for making a coat. – Journeymen ditto £1 and paid for extras. Shoemakers have good wages, and all trades live well. Servant men £30 to £35 per annum. – Servant girls from £16 to £18 per annum. Laborers have 3s. 9d. per day. Beef 3d. per lb. – We can buy it by the quarter for 3½ dollars per 100, that is 100 lbs. for every thing is bought by the pound, not by the stone. Bacon Pigs £5 per 100 lbs. A good goose for 2s. A turkey that weighs 12 lbs. for 2s. 6d. A couple of fowls 1s. 3d. Butter 9d. per lb. Potatoes, 1s. 3d. per bushel. Flour by the barrel, £1s. 5s. – a barrel holds 14 stone,[1] but we shall have it for less in the sleighing time. . . . Tobacco 1s. 3d. per lb. – It has advanced 3d. per lb since I came. Tea from 2s. 4d. to 4s. per lb. Soap 6d. per lb. All other groceries much the same as in England. – Rum 4s per gallon. Best Brandy 7s. 6d. Gin 7s. Wine from 4s. to 8s. per gallon. Whiskey 2s. 6d. – We can buy it from the distillery for 1s. 6d. Ale, by the barrel, 1s. from the brewery; at the tabers, 2s. Good stuff hats, from 3 to 4 dollars. . . .

Colonial Advocate, September 1, 1831.

2) The Society for the Relief of Strangers in Distress

At a General Meeting of the Society for the Relief of Strangers in Distress, held at the Church, this 4th day of April 1820, to receive a Report from the Committee specially appointed to digest a plan for the consideration of the Society, as to the most expedient mode of affording relief and employment to such Emigrants, as may either now, or from time to time be in temporary want of assistance, the following . . . Resolutions as recommended in that Report were unanimously adopted.

Resolved 1st. That as a pecuniary relief, without some return of labor, is but too often productive of idleness, such relief should in future be withheld, except in cases where, from the positive sickness or absence of those of the family capable of manual labor, no means of earning a subsistence remain; provided, the measures proposed for furnishing employment when required should prove attainable.

2d. That the public walk about to be formed near this town, and the projected improvement of the Blue Hill in Yonge Street, appear to offer . . . most desirable opportunities for giving almost immediate employment to any applicants now in want of work.

. . . .

5th . . . That, as a further inducement to the projectors of such works to aid the measure proposed, as well as to prevent any but the really necessitous

[1] a stone equals 14 lbs.

from burthening[1] the Society with unnecessary applications for employ, it becomes highly desirable to fix a maximum of wages at a *lower* rate than what laborers are usually employed at, lest the well meant anxiety of the Society to assist the really distressed should unintentionally operate as an encouragement to the new settlers upon their arrival in the Province, to be dilatory and careless in seeking work from private individuals, or still more injuriously offer a sort of temptation to them to be diverted from their more important ultimate object, namely, that of proceeding to settle upon their new lands.

Upper Canada Gazette, April 13, 1820.

3) **Report on the Petition of the Prisoners in York Gaol**

The Committee, to whom was referred the Petition of the Prisoners in the Gaol of York, setting forth their unfortunate situation, and praying the interference of the House in their behalf, visited the gaol on the fourth day of the present month, examined the Prisoners, enquired into their situation, and have agreed to the following Report.

In the cells below the ground floor, your committee found three female lunatics confined, one of them from England, and who is understood to be the mother of a family, who became deranged on her husband leaving her; another from Ireland, a young woman, and the third a native of Canada. It was stated by the Jailor, that they have as wholesome and nutricious food as himself and family, and there is a stove in the dungeon; but they are lodged in locked up cribs, on straw, two in one crib, and the other by herself; one of them contrived to set fire to the jail some time ago, but it was providentially discovered in time to save the building, by cutting down a door that was in flames. A gentleman confined for debt, complained that the smell from the dungeon in which these poor lunatics are confined, which below the room was almost insupportable, and that their incessant howlings and groans were annoying in the extreme. The smell is certainly most disagreeable, and confinement in such a noisome place, will be likely to aggravate the disorder; who, were they taken to a particular ward in the Hospital, and the usual restraints put upon their persons, (of strait waistcoats,) and gently treated, might either wholly recover their reason, or at least become convalescent. Their confinement is severe beyond that of the most hardened criminal, although their situation entitles them to a double portion of the favorable regard of all in whom the blessing of reason has been bestowed.

Your Committee found 25 persons in this prison, twelve criminals on the ground floor, one criminal sick up stairs, one vagrant, the three lunatics above mentioned, and nine debtors. . . .

The debtors are with one exception, all on the upper floor, apart from the other prisoners. . . . These are allowed no support from their creditors, and some of them say they are entirely without the means of subsistance. James Colquhoun is in jail for a debt of three pounds; the creditor has forgiven the debt, but the lawyer has not thought proper to forgive him fees. Colquhoun

[1] burdening

subsists altogether on the humanity of the jailor and other debtors. One Murphy told your Committee that he had nothing to eat and that both Colquhoun and himself had been for days together, without tasting a morsel.

There are six debtors confined on executions issued out of the Court of King's Bench.

One debtor is in jail, together with his wife, and a family of five children.

Your Committee observed only one person at work; he was a shoemaker.

Your Committee would recommend addressing His Excellency the Lieutenant Governor, requesting the interference of Government on behalf of these prisoners.

A petition to the quarter Sessions, was not, it appears, productive of any good effects.

W. L. Mackenzie,
Chairman.

Committee rooms, Commons
   House of Assembly,
   York, 17th February 1830.

> P.A.O., *Upper Canada, House of Assembly*, Journals, 1830, Appendix, p. 162.

4) The Upper Class

The public amusements in Toronto[1] are not of a nature to attract much attention. There have been various attempts to get up respectable races, and to establish a theatre, and a winter assembly for dancing; but owing to the peculiar state of society, these attempts have always proved nearly abortive, as well as those of a much higher and more useful kind, which have been made by persons attached to science and the arts. A national Literary and Philosophical Society was by great exertion established; but, after being in a wavering state for about a year, it dropped. The United Service Club met with the same fate; and there is now only a Mechanics' Institute, and a commercial news-room, which can fairly be mentioned, although some young men, under the patronage of the Vice-Chancellor, have recently got up a literary club.

In Toronto, which has only advanced rapidly within the last five years, the original settlers were chiefly persons holding public appointments, whose duty obliged them to reside at the seat of government. Tradesmen, mechanics, and labourers came to the village by very slow degrees; and, as they were chiefly concerned in supplying the wants of the gentry, were not until recently, enabled to amass much money. Thus, a very clear and defined line was drawn in the society of York; and, as the families of the office-holders became connected by marriage (for York was not sought as a place of residence by general settlers in the country, and was chiefly visited by them on public business), a close and impenetrable bond of union arose among these public servants; and the aristocracy of Little York was able to carve out at will the destinies of the town, naturally endeavouring to retain in the family compact all situations of

---

[1] York was renamed Toronto in 1834.

honour and profit. They were, however, too few to establish, however willing, any useful public institutions; and hence, when the place became a city, and wealth and intellect flowed into it from foreign sources, a little jealousy would obviously, for some time, prevent these self-constituted leaders from patronizing efforts made by strangers.

R. H. Bonnycastle, *The Canadas in 1841* (London, 1841), vol. I, pp. 168-170.

7.   Land Policies

1. What does the advertisement for the Canada Company tell you about this company?

2. By examining the problems which settlers faced before the Company was organized, estimate the service it offered to settlers.

3. What were the terms by which settlers purchased Crown land? By referring to the document on page 99, suggest why many farmers would consider armed rebellion.

4. On what basis was the government's land policy criticized?

1) Advertisement for the Canada Company

Have for sale in Upper Canada, about two millions, five hundred acres of Land, of the following description.

First, CROWN RESERVES; being Lots of 200 Acres each; scattered throughout the older Townships of the Province.

Second, BLOCKS OF LAND; of, from 1000 to 40,000 acres. – These are situated in the Townships of the Western District, and in the township of Wilmot in the Gore District.

Third, A Town and Township called GUELPH in the GORE DISTRICT, in which there are already nearly 800 Settlers; with almost every kind of tradesmen and Mechanicks: Taverns, Stores, Schools, Saw Mills &c. and a Grist-Mill is in progress. This is a desirable location for settlers with small Capitals, as laborers and Servants are easily procurable; and lots, partly improved, can be purchased at a reasonable price.

Fourth, THE HURON TERRITORY, containing one million, one hundred thousand acres. In the shape of a triangle, the base resting for upwards of sixty miles, on the bank of Lake Huron.

The Town of Goderich has been commenced on the side of a harbor, formed by the confluence of the river Maitland and the Lake; and as a road is already cut to the Gore District; and another is in progress to the London District, it has already become the centre of Settlement. There are already about 500 inhabitants in the Huron tract – a Saw Mill is in operation – and a Grist Mill building – several Taverns and Stores have been established; and a brewery and Distillery are in progress.

The Land is admitted on all hands to be equal to any in the province – it possesses lime, and building stone – brick earth, and potters clay, in abundance; and the produce of the country can be carried to market by water, through Lake Huron, by the river St. Clair, to the Lakes Erie, and Ontario, and the River St. Lawrence, to Montreal and Quebec.

Niagara Herald, May 20, 1830.

2) Aid to Settlers

But to those who mean to purchase lands from the Company, all care upon the subject of travelling expenses is obviated by a liberal and proper arrangement, which is published for the information of emigrants, as follows:–

The Company's agents, on the arrival of emigrants at Quebec or Montreal, will, for the season of 1832, convey them, *free of expense*, To York, or the head of lake Ontario, which is in the vicinity of their choicest lands, *provided the emigrants pay a first instalment in London, Quebec, or Montreal*, of two shillings an acre, upon not less than one hundred acres; and the Company's agents, in all parts of the Upper Province, will give such emigrants every information and assistance in their power. . . .

A. Pickens, *The Canadas* (London, 1832), p. 255.

3) Crown Lands

Sale of Crown Lands

Notice is hereby given, that a portion of the Vacant Lots in the Town of Chatham, in the Western District, will be exposed to sale by Public Auction, at the Inn of Claude Cartier, in the Town of Chatham, on Thursday the 1st November next, at

10 o'clock, A.M.
on the following conditions,
– VIZ: –

The *Purchase Money* to be paid by Four Instalments, with Interest; the First Instalment at the time of Sale, and the Second, Third and Fourth Instalments, at the interval of a year between each, and subject to the condition of building a Stone, Brick, or Frame House, not less than 24 Feet long and 18 Feet wide, to be completed within two years from the day of Sale.

Peter Robinson.

Commissioner of Crown Lands Office,
    York, 24th Sept. 1832.

Niagara Gleaner, October 20, 1832.

4) Lord Durham's Criticism of the Land Grant System

In Upper Canada, 3,200,000 acres have been granted to "U. E. Loyalists," being refugees from the United States who settled in the Province before 1787, and their children; 730,000 acres to militiamen, 450,000 acres to discharged soldiers and sailors, 255,000 acres to magistrates and barristers, 136,000 acres to executive councillors and their families, 50,000 acres to five legislative councillors and their families, 36,900 acres to clergymen as private property, 264,000 acres to persons contracting to make surveys, 95,526 acres to officers of the army and navy, 500,000 acres for the endowment of schools, 48,520 acres to Colonel Talbot, 12,000 acres to the heirs of General Brock, and 12,000 acres to Doctor Mountain, a former Bishop of Quebec; making altogether, with the clergy reserves, nearly half of all the surveyed land in the Province. . . .

In Upper Canada, a very small proportion (perhaps less than a tenth) of the land thus granted has been even occupied by settlers, much less reclaimed and cultivated. . . .

No other result could have been expected in the case of those classes of grantees whose station would preclude them from settling in the wilderness, and whose means would enable them to avoid exertion for giving immediate value to their grants; and, unfortunately, the land which was intended for persons of a poorer order, who might be expected to improve it by their labour, has, for the most part, fallen into the hands of land-jobbers of the class just mentioned, who have never thought of settling in person, and who retain the land in its present wild state, speculating upon its acquiring a value at some distant day, when the demand for land shall have increased through the increase in population.

G. M. Craig, ed., *Lord Durham's Report* (Toronto: McClelland and Stewart, 1963), pp. 118-119.

8.   The Bank of Upper Canada

1. What financial problems impeded Upper Canada before 1815? (see pp. 40-44)

2. By examining the first source, determine the contribution of the Bank of Upper Canada to the progress of the Province.

3. Why did Mackenzie object to the idea of banks?

4. How might the depression of 1833-1837 have contributed to rebellion?

1) H. J. Boulton[1] to R. J. W. Horton[2]

... In 1819 the Bank of U Canada the only Institution of the kind in that Province was first chartered by Act of the Provl. Parlt. with a joint Stock Capital of £200,000 which being found larger than the state of the Colony required was by a subsequent Statute reduced one half – ....

With this Constitution the Bank began Business in 1821 & have continued ever since in a state of successful operation netting after the first year from 8 to 12 Per Ct. Profit upon the Capital Paid –

The Confidence of the Public is unbounded and the Notes of the U. C. Bank are current along the whole line of the American frontier bordering on Canada and are only at a small discount in New York and this owing to the Commercial relations of the two Countries & not to any distrust in the soundness of the Institution –

. . . .

[The Bank] has acquired a degree of stability which probably exceeds that of most Banking Institutions in America. The Circulation is now upwards of £70,000 and its Capital paid in about half that amount; probably £50,000 of this is afloat in U Canada and the residue abroad in the U States & Lower Canada – Almost the only Specie[3] that finds its way into U Canada is that which is issued by the Commissariat to the Troops. ...

P.A.O., Colonial Office 42, U376, pp. 163-164.

2) Mackenzie's Criticism of the Bank

There can be no doubt but that the government officers, in their anxious chase after money, wealth, power, will strain every nerve to get a bill passed during the present session to allow them to circulate exclusively another million of their paper dollars at the expense of the country, and it may be to its lasting injury, but assuredly for their own individual advantage. Even now, by keeping up a monopoly of the rate of interest on government loans, and on loans to districts, they gain nearly £5,000 a year out of the very poverty of the people. ... they can raise the price of property or lower it at will, by increasing, or withdrawing from circulation, their paper money. They cannot, say some, influence the vote of members of the assembly – but they can ruin them and break their bank credit if they do not vote to suit the interests of those who control the money loans. They cannot vote at elections, but they can punish mercantile people if their votes and exertions are not directed in favour of candidates who would sell the rights of the people for a mess of pottage.

Colonial Advocate, November 17, 1831.

[1] Henry Boulton held a number of governmental positions before his election to the Assembly in 1830. He was also the solicitor for the Bank of Upper Canada for a number of years.

[2] Robert Horton was Under-Secretary of State for War and the Colonies, 1821-1828.

[3] Hard currency, either gold or silver.

3) Depression 1833-1837

COMMERCIAL DISTRESS. — The inhabitants of Toronto, we believe, never before nor since it was a city, have experienced any thing like the depression in business which this spring has produced. There are, upon every hand, day after day failures, even of persons who were formerly considered in at least comfortable circumstances. And to what can this be owing? We pretend not to know the minutiae of the matter, but should be inclined to think that a deficiency in the circulating medium, however caused, has led to the destruction of many persons possessed of property more than sufficient to cover any demand that might be made against them, but who could not raise the ready means, at the moment by which those demands could be answered.

Montreal Gazette, May 23, 1835.

9.   Were religious forces active?

1. After reviewing the section on religion (pages 58-64), restate the religious conflicts and issues which existed before 1812.

2. What are the issues described by Anson Green?

3. Does Green have a bias? Why?

4. Why would the Methodists find strong support in the Legislative Assembly?

5. How might the religious issues described below contribute to feelings of rebellion?

6. What were the Clergy Reserves? Why might the phrase "Protestant Clergy" cause problems?

1) A Methodist Preacher examines Religious Conflict

. . . I desire . . . to give a brief outline of the former struggles of our Church for religious freedom. . . . The Methodist Church seems to have been the principal object of the crushing influence of the Family Compact — not because we were more sincere and determined in our opposition to an Established Church in Canada than our brethren of other communions, but because we were more numerous and more powerful than they. . . . Dr. Strachan was a member of both our Legislative and Executive Councils. He went to England to obtain a charter for a sectarian[1] college to be heavily endowed from public lands. To accomplish this, he prepared what he called an "Ecclesiastical Chart" of this Province, and on the 16th of May, 1827, sent it to Lord Goderich, the Colonial Secretary. . . . When it reached this country it was found to be so strangely inaccurate and one-sided that it occasioned a general outburst of

[1] devoted to a sect

disgust from one end of the Province to the other. He gave credit for one decent Methodist preacher, two Presbyterians, and three or four Congregationalists. The others were mostly aliens, capable of "rendering a large portion of the country hostile to our institutions, both civil and religious." And the only way to prevent this awful catastrophe was by increasing the number of what he was pleased to call the "Established Clergy!" Liberal-minded men of all Churches in York prepared a memorial and sent it through the country for signatures, asking the Parliament to institute a public investigation. . . . The House appointed a large Committee, and examined no less than fifty-two gentlemen, embracing all shades of politics and religion, who, with remarkable unanimity, pronounced the Chart strangely at variance with truth, or opposed to obvious facts. The Committee made a full report to Parliament, condemning the Chart in the strongest terms. . . . "The insinuations in the letter against the Methodist Clergymen the Committee have noticed with peculiar regret. . . . Their ministry and instructions, far from having, as is represented in the letter, a tendency hostile to our institutions, have been conducive – in a degree which cannot be easily estimated – to the reformation of their hearers from licentiousness and to the diffusion of correct morals – the foundation of all sound loyalty and social order. There is reason to believe that, as a body, they have not failed to inculcate, by precept and example, as a Christian duty, an attachment to the Sovereign, and a cheerful and conscientious obedience to the laws of the country. . . . No one doubts that the Methodists are as loyal as any other of His Majesty's subjects. And the very fact that, while their clergymen are dependant for their support upon the voluntary contributions of their people, the number of their members – in the opinion of almost all the witnesses – has increased so as to be now greater than that of the members of any other denomination in the Province, *is a complete refutation* of any suspicion that their influence and instructions have such a tendency."

In addition to this able report, the House sent an address to King George, in which they say:– "We have seen with equal surprise and regret a letter and Chart, dated 16th May, 1827, and addressed by the Hon. and Venerable Dr. Strachan, Archdeacon of York, a member of Your Majesty's Legislative and Executive Councils of this Province, to the Right Hon. R. J. Wilmot Horton, as they are inaccurate in some important respects, and are calculated to lead Your Majesty's Government into serious errors. Of Your Majesty's subjects in this Province, *only a small part* are members of the Church of England; and there is not any particular tendency to that Church among the people, and nothing could cause more alarm and grief in their minds than the apprehension that there was a design on the part of Your Majesty's Government to establish, as a part of the State, one or more Churches or denominations of Christians in this Province. We are convinced that the tendency of their influence and instruction is not hostile to our institutions, but, on the contrary, is eminently favourable to religion and morality; and their labours are calculated to make their people better men and better subjects, and have already produced in this Province the happiest effects."

Anson Green, *Life and Times of Anson Green* (Toronto, 1877), pp. pp. 128-131.

2) The Clergy Reserves

The episcopal form of religion, according to the establishment of the Church of England, is supported by the government of this province. The constitutional act provided for a reservation of lands equal to one seventh part of all the lands then granted, and to be granted. These reserves, altogether distinct and different from those of another seventh, called the crown reserves, were required to be specified in the patents, and are appropriated exclusively to the maintenance of a Protestant clergy in the province.

> Robert Gourley, *Statistical Account of Upper Canada* (London, 1822), I, pp. 2131-232.

10. Did any new technological developments influence the situation?

In this, our technological age, when we can send men to the moon, see war as it really is in our own living rooms, and fly across continents in three hours, we tend to accept technology as a way of life. But it is interesting to speculate how history might have been altered if the printing press had not been invented when Luther broke with the Catholic church; if the atomic bomb had first been discovered by the Germans or if television was unable to cover the war in Vietnam, riots in American cities, or American and Canadian elections.

The nineteenth century was an era of rapid technological change, particularly in Britain, where in 1837, the Industrial Revolution was gaining momentum. In Canada, despite its backwardness, technology was making an impression.

1. After examining an Atlas, suggest the purpose of the Welland Canal. Why would a number of locks be necessary?

2. Why would the government support such a commercial venture?

3. Based on Mackenzie's criticism of the canals, why might small farmers object to the government's canal building programme?

1) The Welland Canal

WELLAND CANAL. – DEPARTURE OF THE FIRST VESSEL. – Saturday last was a proud day for St. Catharines; and indeed, for Upper Canada. A scene was witnessed within its borders, that will long be held in remembrance by the active friends and steady supporters of the splendid plans of internal improvement now in progress in this section of the colony – the free and uninterrupted passage of the first loaded vessel, that ever floated on the waters of the Welland Canal, from this village to lake Ontario, a distance of five miles of artificial Steam Boat Navigation, constructed up the valley of the 12 mile creek, directly into the interior of the country. A scene which was at once, so grand, so novel and interesting, as to call forth the spontaneous acclamations of every liberal and patriotic spectator assembled on the joyous occasion.

It was a matter of sincere regret to many, that the projector of this great work[1] was not present – being now in London endeavouring to procure the necessary means for its completion to Lake Erie; and there can be little doubt but his efforts will be crowned with success.

Montreal Gazette, June 5, 1828.

2) Mackenzie's Election Programme

That laying out many thousand pounds for making a ship navigation, chiefly for naval and military purposes, in one corner of the province, called the Welland Canal, while no effectual aid has been afforded to repair the roads and bridges of this district, and while the far more important navigation of the St. Lawrence remains unimproved, is contrary to sound policy and unjust towards this neglected part of the colony.

Colonial Advocate, January 31, 1828.

11.   Can the events be partially explained by weakened or strengthened institutions?

What do the Y.W.C.A., the Boy Scouts, the Catholic church, the New Democratic Party and the Canadian Manufacturers Association have in common? While dissimilar in purpose and structure, each of these is an institution. In broad terms an institution is an organization formed around a certain set of ideas and values, which expresses the views of its members and enforces a degree of cooperation and conformity upon them. Such an organization, the "Family Compact," will be examined in order to determine its role in causing the rebellion.

1. How does Lord Durham define the "Family Compact"? How does Head define this institution? To what extent do they agree or disagree?

[1] William Hamilton Merritt, son of Loyalist parents, was the promoter of the Welland canal.

2. After doing some research on the careers of Durham and Head, account for their differing opinions on the "Family Compact."

3. Does the "Family Compact" conform to our definition of an institution?

4. What characteristics does the local "Family Compact" share with the institution described by Durham and Head? Why did a large percentage of the settlers on Talbot's land grant rebel in 1837?

1) Lord Durham's Opinion

Upper Canada . . . has long been entirely governed by a party, commonly designated throughout the province as the Family Compact, a name not much more appropriate than party designations usually are, inasmuch as there is, in truth, very little of family connection among persons thus united. For a long time, this body of men, receiving at times accession[1] to its members, possessed almost all the highest public offices, by means of which, and of its influence in the Executive Council, it wielded all the powers of government; it maintained influence in the Legislature by means of its predominance in the Legislative Council; and it disposed of the large number of petty[2] posts which are the patronage of the Government all over the Province. Successive Governors, as they came in their turn, are said to have either submitted quietly to its influence, or after a short and unavailing struggle to have yielded to this well-organized party the real conduct of affairs. . . the magistracy, the highest offices of the Episcopal Church,[3] and a great part of the legal profession are filled by the adherents of this party: by grant or purchase they have acquired nearly the whole of the waste lands of the Province: they are all powerful in the chartered banks, and till lately, shared among themselves almost exclusively all offices of trust and profit. The bulk of this party consists, for the most part of native born inhabitants of the Colony, or of emigrants who settled in it before the last war with the United States; the principal members of it belong to the Church of England, and the maintenance of the claims of that church has always been one of its distinguishing characteristics.

G. M. Craig, *op. cit.*, pp. 79-80.

2) Sir Francis Bond Head's Point of View

It appears from Lord Durham's own showing, that the "Family Compact" which his Lordship deems so advisable that the Queen should destroy, is nothing more or less than that "social fabric" which characterizes every civilized community in the world. It is that social fabric, or rather, fortress within which the British yeoman,[4] farmer, and manufacturer is enabled to repel the extortionate demands of his labourers; and to preserve from pillage and robbery the harvest of his industry after he has reaped it.

[1] An increase.
[2] Minor.
[3] Church of England.
[4] A small landowner.

. . . , 'the magistrates,' 'the clergy,' 'the landed proprietors,' 'the bankers,' 'the native-born inhabitants,' and 'the supporters of the Established Church,' form just as much 'a family compact' in England as they do in Upper Canada and just as much in Germany as they do in England. . . .

The Family Compact of Upper Canada is composed of those members of its society who, either by their abilities of character have been honoured by the confidence of the executive government, or who, by their industry and intelligence, have amassed wealth. The party, I own, is comparatively a small one; but to put the multitude at the top and the few at the bottom is a radical reversion of the pyramid of society which every reflecting man must foresee, can end only by its downfall.

Sir F. B. Head, *A Narrative* (London, 1839), pp. 464-465.

3) A Local Family Compact

The county of Middlesex, from its first settlement up to this moment, has been controlled . . . as absolutely and despotically as is the petty sovereignty of a German despot. This they have been enabled to do through the immense influence their high official stations give them. Magistrates, officers of the excise, surveyors, militia officers, commissioners to carry the appropriations of public money into effect, all are appointed through the recommendations and influence of these sages of the District – thus forming a host of worthies who are ever at the beck of their Patrons. We assert without fear of contradiction, that the Hon. Colonel Talbot rules with a more absolute sway, and his power is infinitely more to be dreaded than that of the King of Great Britain. . . . It is the fear of this Iron rule that has controlled our former elections. . . .

St. Thomas Liberal, July 25, 1833.

12. Was physical environment a factor in the situation?

In many ways, Canadian history has been determined by geography. In fact, some of Canada's most important historians argue that most major Canadian events are, in large measure, the result of the attempt of Canadians to turn the St. Lawrence and Great Lakes systems into a great inland trade network. The first document provides the geographical explanation for the government's support of a canal system. The second reveals why a rebel who had spent a lifetime fighting the physical environment, only to lose his life in 1837, would support rebellion.

1. From previous sources provide evidence to demonstrate the influence of the physical environment upon life in Upper Canada.

2. Suggest the role which the promoters of the Welland Canal saw for it in attracting the inland trade of North America?

3. How has environment shaped the attitudes of the farmer quoted in document two?

1) The Welland Canal and the Commercial Empire of the St. Lawrence

We are informed by a gentleman who has just visited the Welland Canal, that from a rough calculation, he supposes 300,000 staves have already been brought through it. This is a new article of exportation from Lake Erie and must have been new in centuries to come but for the Canal. It is painful, however, to reflect that the Americans are nearly, if not quite, the sole carriers of Lumber and Staves from the head of the Lake to Quebec and Montreal. Somebody must be off their guard to allow this. The cause should be immediately sought for, and a remedy applied. We hope those immediately interested, will bestir themselves and take proper steps to abate so vile a nuisance. We understand the quantity of White Oak on the shores of Lake Erie, and in the Michigan Territory, is prodigously great, the whole of which, is now open to a market; but in the name of common sense, let us not throw away the bread which a kind providence has put into our mouths.

Montreal Gazette, August 16, 1830.

2) Testimony of a Western Ontario Rebel

The author has been in Canada since he was a little boy, and he has not had the advantage of a classical education at the King's College,[1] or the less advantages derived from a District School. The greater part of his time has been spent watching over and providing for an increasing and tender family. He had in most instances to make his own roads and bridges, clear his own farm, educate himself and his children, be his own mechanic, and except now and then, he had no society but his own family. He had his bones broken by the fall of trees, his feet lacerated by the axe, and suffered almost everything except death. He waited year after year in hope of better days, expecting that the government would care less for themselves and more for the people. But every year he has been disappointed.

Robert Davis, *The Canadian Farmer's Travels in the U.S.A.* (Buffalo, 1860), pp. 3-4.

[1] King's College, now part of the University of Toronto, founded by John Strachan.

13.   The Rebellion Unfolds

Joseph Richard Thompson has left students of the rebellion an interesting and useful look at the rebellion period as seen through the eyes of a resident of the back townships. Thompson, a lawyer, lived south east of Lake Simcoe, approximately sixty miles from Toronto.

1. Why did most back country people remain loyal? What was their chief concern upon learning of the rebellion?

2. Account for the fact that neither Mackenzie nor his principles are mentioned.

3. What does this source reveal about communications in 1837?

4. Who were Orangemen? How did they influence the suppression of the rebellion?

5. Why would a man like Thompson keep such a close record of events?

1) 1837.

Decr. 5. Went to Bagshaw's for letters & newspapers recd. the "Const^n."[1] "Albion."[2]

Bagshaw asked me some mysterious questions respecting the departure of some of our neighbours which I could not comprehend.

. . . .

6. This morning he & W Cowan came in while we were at breakfast with the intelligence that several of our neighbours had gone into Toronto to have a hand with other bodies of men in taking the City & getting possession of the 6000 arms in it.

. . . .

7. This morning while at breakfast M. Cowan came in breathless to tell us that Lieut. Gibbs had just arrived with orders for all persons to proceed to Newmarket to join with a party going to Toronto – that the Governor was taken prisoner together with the Garrison.

. . . .

Arranged with Gibbs that a public Meeting of the Inhabitants sh^d. be held the next morning for adopting measures to protect property & preserve peace.

. . . .

On my return found that news had arrived that the Lieut-Govr. was killed the Garrison not taken & Toronto blockaded.

[1] Mackenzie's paper, *Constitution*, was last published on November 29, 1837.

[2] Published in New York, *Albion*, was quite influential in Upper Canada.

8. This morning there was a meeting of about 40 persons at our house, who after some discussion, concurred in the propriety of forming a Society to protect property & preserve the peace & signed a Document agreeing thereto. . . .

One report is that 5000 Americans from the U.S. have come over & assisted in the capture of Toronto.

One affirms that only 7 lives have been lost – another that there are heaps of slain – it is said that the L[t]. Governor was taken in a boat while endeavouring to cross to the U.S.

In the night two persons brought word to Cowan's that Toronto was not taken, with some other information. . . .

9. In the afternoon Henry Edwards called on us and brought fresh news – The son of a Captain Logie of Ops had left Toronto on Wednesday – the last person he spoke to on that day was the son of the L[t]. Governor, who was superintending the fortifying of the Bank of U.C. at that time Toronto was quite safe – strongly fortified & protected by bodies of whites and blacks[1] – several steamers in the Lake to prevent persons approaching from the U.S. Further on Monday the L[t]. Gov[r]. was occupied in distributing arms to the inhabitants & swearing them in to keep the peace – the same evening an attack was made which was unsuccessful, & the party attacking were still near & around the city but no danger from them was apprehended on the contrary the L[t]. Governor in a speech delivered in the public stret had recommended that the settlers in the Back Townships sh[d]. unite themselves to protect property & maintain order, as there was more danger to be apprehended *there* than in Toronto.

In the evening W. Cowan called & it appeared from what he had heard that there was actually danger of the back settlers having their property or lives attacked.

On that evening we secured the doors & windows & had our fire arms ready loaded.

10. . . . . I learn that all was safe on the road to Toronto by Whitby, & that the Inhabitants of the front were alarmed by reports that the Indians had risen in the back settlements and were burning & massacreing all before them.

12. It is reported that several persons from this neighbourhood have been killed in the tumults of the week . . .

13. . . . K. McCaskill & I. McKay came & informed me that they brought unpleasant news – that a mob of orangemen were going about threatening to burn down the houses of such persons as they chose to visit – carrying away fire arms &c.

19. . . . . I this day for the first time saw in the Xian Guardians[2] of the 6th & 13th inst. the full particulars of the late disturbances.

During the week numerous parties of armed men have been observed passing our house & several more prisoners have been taken.

From this day to the 1st January nothing of moment has occurred.

[1] Runaway slaves, fearful of American support for Mackenzie, supported the government.
[2] *Christian Guardian* was the newspaper of the Methodist church.

On the 4th. January I went to the Post office and there procured for the 1st. time a copy of the Lieut. Governor's speech made on 28th. Decr. on opening the session. The Post this evening also brought the Patriot[1] of the 2d. January giving an acct. of the destruction of the Steam boat Caroline which was proceeding from Buffalo to Navy Island laden with provisions &c.

. . . it was determined that I shd. proceed to Toronto ascertain the real state of affairs & if necessary to offer ourselves as volunteers in repelling the invasion of this country by American citizens.

On the 9th. I accordingly started & reached Uxbridge that evening – the next day I proceeded to Markham where I found that the Militia had just been summoned to proceed to Yonge St. About 30 marched off that night and all night parties kept arriving. No one knew the cause of the summons.

On the 11th. I reached Toronto when I learned that the cause of the Militia having been called out was a report that the rebels had assembled near Newmarket & were about to release the prisoners in Toronto. On the 12th. I went to the Lieut. Governor's & was informed that at present no further volunteers were required, and that if circumstances shd. call for the people in the Back Townships to come forward a special Messenger would be despatched to inform them.

. . . .

I remained in Toronto until the 17th. during which time I had a opportunity of seeing several of the U.S. papers, and observing the extraordinary endeavours made by them to excite the people agst. the British.

I also had an opportunity of hearing some interesting anecdotes relative to the events at the Government House on the night of the 5th. Decr. related by an eyewitness.

On the night of the 17th. I reached the Lord Nelson near Markham – the next day Uxbridge . . . The next day the 19th. I reached home.

Nothing occurred until the 25th. when a Meeting took place at Cowan's at which 217 persons took the oath of allegiance & enrolled themselves in the Militia Regt. of Brock.

> C. P. Stacey, "The Crisis of 1837 in a Back Township of Upper Canada," *Canadian Historical Review*, XI, (1930), pp. 223-232.

14. The Aftermath of Rebellion to 1841

When Mackenzie fled to the United States, his unsuccessful, and somewhat comical rebellion, left Upper Canada politically and socially divided. While men debated the fate of the hundreds of imprisoned rebels, the "Family Compact" relaxed, satisfied that

[1] *Toronto Patriot* was a strong supporter of the government.

the rebellion had justified its actions. Meanwhile, the reformers, in an attempt to resurrect their fortunes, dissociated themselves from the rebels, who they had denounced as irresponsible malcontents as early as 1832. This was the situation Lord Durham found in Upper Canada in 1838. Appointed by Britain as Governor-General of the Canadas and High Commissioner to investigate the disorders, Durham spent less than a year in Canada and only five days in Upper Canada. But his famous report, published in 1839, had a far reaching impact upon Upper Canada.

1. Compare Durham's recommendation in section one to Robert Baldwin's views concerning government on page 90.

2. What advantage does Durham see in union with Lower Canada?

3. To what extent were Durham's recommendations concerning Upper Canada carried out?

1) Lord Durham's Report
A Governmental Recommendation

. . . . It needs no change in the principles of government, no invention of a new constitutional theory, to supply the remedy which would, in my opinion, completely remove the existing political disorders. It needs but to follow out consistently the principles of the British Constitution, and introduce into the Government of these great Colonies those wise provisions, by which alone the working of the representative system can in any country be rendered harmonious and efficient. We are not now to consider the policy of establishing representative government in the North American Colonies. . . . To conduct their Government harmoniously, in accordance with its established principles, is now the business of its rulers; and I know not how it is possible to secure that harmony in any other way, than by administering the Government on those principles which have been found perfectly efficacious in Great Britain. I would not impair a single prerogative of the Crown; on the contrary, I believe that the interests of the people of these Colonies require the protection of prerogatives, which have not hitherto been exercised. But the Crown must, on the other hand, submit to the necessary consequences of representative institutions; and if it has to carry on the Government in unison with a representative body, it must consent to carry it on by means of those in whom that representative body has confidence.

. . . .

G. M. Craig, ed., *op. cit.*, p. 139.

2) Union for Upper Canada

The union of the two Provinces would secure to Upper Canada the present great objects of its desire. All disputes as to the division or amount of the revenue would cease. The surplus revenue of Lower Canada would supply the deficiency of that part of the upper Province; and the Province thus placed beyond the possibility of locally jobbing the surplus revenue, which it cannot reduce, would, I think, gain as much by the arrangement as the Province, which would thus find a means of paying the interest of its debt. Indeed it would be by no means unjust to place this burthen on Lower Canada, inasmuch as the great public works for which the debt was contracted, are as much the concern of one Province as of the other. Nor is it to be supposed that, whatever may have been the mismanagement, in which a great part of the debt originated, the canals of Upper Canada will always be a source of loss, instead of profit. The completion of the projected and necessary line of public works would be promoted by such a union. The access to the sea would be secured to Upper Canada. The saving of public money, which would be ensured by the union of various establishments in the two Provinces, would supply the means of conducting the general Government on a more efficient scale than it has yet been carried on. And the responsibility of the executive would be secured by the increased weight which the representative body of the United Province would bring to bear on the Imperial Government and legislature.

Ibid., pp. 159-160.

---

15.   Reaction to Durham's Report

1. Account for John Beverley Robinson's[1] violent denunciation of Durham's report.

2. According to Lieutenant Governor Arthur,[2] how did Durham's report affect party alignments? Who organized the Durham meetings? Why?

1) J. B. Robinson to Arthur, Feb. 19, 1839

I had not then seen the Report – I have since carefully perused it – You have had a Copy sent to you I know – and need I say to you or to any honest man who has spent three months in Upper Canada that *all* that relates to that Province is disgraceful & mischievous – It absolutely made me ill, to read it – You said rightly to me once "Lord Durham is a bad man" – I should try in vain to find words to express the contempt I feel for him – after what I have heard him say – & after what he is known to have said to others – . . . . If the legre.[3] & people – or the people of U C. favor the union of the two Provinces I think it will take place – & it may, whether they do or not – I am convinced it would

---

[1] Attorney General of Upper Canada and a leading member of the "Family Compact."
[2] Sir George Arthur replaced Sir Francis Bond Head as Lieutenant-Governor in 1838, only to be replaced by Lord Sydenham in 1839.
[3] Legislature.

be the ruin of both Colonies – . . . . I shall devote my whole time to the efforts ne[ce]ssa[r]y for counteracting as much as possible the evil that may be feared from Ld. Durham's report – for leading the Governmt into a right course for the future governmt of Canada & for providing by a series of Executive & Legislative measures for the security of Canada agt. our lawless neighbours – . . . .

> C. R. Sanderson, ed., *The Arthur Papers*, II (Toronto: Toronto Public Libraries, 1957), pp. 47-48.

2) Arthur to Colborne,[1] Aug. 8, 1839

The Durham Meetings are in high repute, and the cry is down with the "Family Compact," & hurrah for a responsible Governt – . In fact, Lord Durham's Mission seems to have filled up the Measure of Woe in Upper Canada. Whilst the Conflict was between the Constitutional party & the Reformers, there was every thing to hope, and I vainly supposed that there was a good prospect of better days – but, with matchless imprudence the high Commissioner has proposed a Measure which has divided the Loyal Party, & thereby given a vast preponderance to the Republicans – which must turn the scale in their favor at the next Election. Throughout the Country there is a worse spirit than has prevailed since the outbreak in December 1837; and I am persuaded the worst days are to come. A Spark was enough to kindle a flame & Lord Durham has thrown a firebrand amongst the People. I do not say this in bad spirit for I do believe He intended well but never was any person more mistaken, or more misinformed.

> *Ibid.*, II, p. 207.

The End of an Era

In February, 1841, the Act of Union became effective. With it, an era of Canadian history ended. The simple uncomplicated way of life which characterized the pre-rebellion period disappeared as Upper Canada lost its separate identity and Canadians became caught up in railways, early industrialism, political deadlock and in 1867, Confederation.

From its primitive, halting beginnings in the 1780's and 1790's Upper Canada by 1841, had emerged as a "relatively mature and complex community – the base from which English speaking civilization developed into central and western Canada."[2] This society, which had developed towns and cities, constructed roads and canals, solidified religious and educational institutions, and adopted paths of political moderation rather than radicalism, blended a unique combination of British and American values, attitudes and institutions into the definitive Canadian character with which the province went forward into the next half century.

[1] Sir John Colborne, former Lieutenant Governor of Upper Canada.
[2] Craig, *Upper Canada*, p. xiii.

Topics for Further Inquiry

1. By applying the approach to causation outlined in Part three, briefly suggest the possible causes of either Confederation in 1867, or the Northwest Rebellion of 1885.

2. Choose one of the following individuals, and construct a four page argument to support one of the two interpretations of each:
   a. Robert Baldwin: Great Statesman or "man of one policy."
   b. Robert Gourlay: martyred patriot or irresponsible agitator.
   c. William Lyon Mackenzie: patriot or rebel.
   d. John Strachan: misguided fanatic or stabilizing influence.

3. Describe the development of the Upper Canadian economy from 1784 to 1837.

4. Describe the evolution of education in Upper Canada from 1784 to 1837.

5. By examining religion in Upper Canada from 1784 to 1837, determine its role and influence in the community.

Bibliographical Note

G. M. Craig's *Upper Canada: The Formative Years* contains a comprehensive bibliography of both primary and secondary sources. Students will also find the following titles from McClelland and Stewart's *Carleton Library Series* valuable:

G. M. Craig   *Lord Durham's Report.*
Chester New   *Lord Durham's Mission to Canada, 1815–1836.*
Fred Landon   *Western Ontario and The American Frontier.*
Peter Burroughs   *The Colonial Reformers and Canada, 1830–1849.*
J. L. H. Henderson   *John Strachan: Documents and Opinions.*
S. F. Wise   *A Narrative by Sir Francis Bond Head.*

William Kilbourn's excellent biography of William Lyon Mackenzie, *The Firebrand* (Toronto: Clarke Irwin, 1956), is also highly recommended for students of the Rebellion period.

In addition, the Ontario Historical Society's publication *Ontario History* and the Champlain Society's publications supply useful sources for further research. Local historical societies in Ontario often provide helpful publications. The addresses of these societies are listed in *Ontario History*.

Acknowledgements

This page constitutes an extension of the copyright page. For permission to reprint copyright material, grateful acknowledgement is made to the following:

THE BURLINGTON LOCAL HISTORY PROJECT, Ontario, for extracts from *A Geographical View of the Province of Upper Canada* by M. Smith.

CANADIAN HISTORICAL REVIEW, University of Toronto Press, for the extract from the article "The Crisis of 1837 in a Back Township of Upper Canada" by C. P. Stacey.

THE HISTORICAL MAGAZINE OF THE PROTESTANT EPISCOPAL CHURCH, Austin, Texas, for permission to reprint *The Reverend John Stuart. Missionary to the Mohawks* by J. W. Lydekker.

THE McGRAW-HILL BOOK COMPANY, New York, for the extract from *A Preface to History* by C. G. Gustavson. Used with permission of McGraw-Hill Book Company.

THE NIAGARA HISTORICAL SOCIETY, Ontario, for permission to quote from *Extract from a letter from Lieut. Governor Hope to the Commissioners for American claims.*

THE ONTARIO HISTORICAL SOCIETY, Toronto, for extracts from *The Correspondence of Lieutenant Governor John Graves Simcoe*, by E. A. Cruikshank ed., and for the extract from *The Government of Upper Canada and Robert Gourlay: Illustrated Documents, 1814-1821*, by E. A. Cruikshank ed.

THE ONTARIO SYNOD OF THE ANGLICAN CHURCH, Kingston, Ontario, for permission to reprint excerpts from *The Stuart Papers*.

UNIVERSITY OF TORONTO PRESS, for an extract from *Select Documents in Canadian Economic History 1783-1885* eds. H. A. Innis and A. R. M. Lower.